Making and Decorating Pottery Tiles

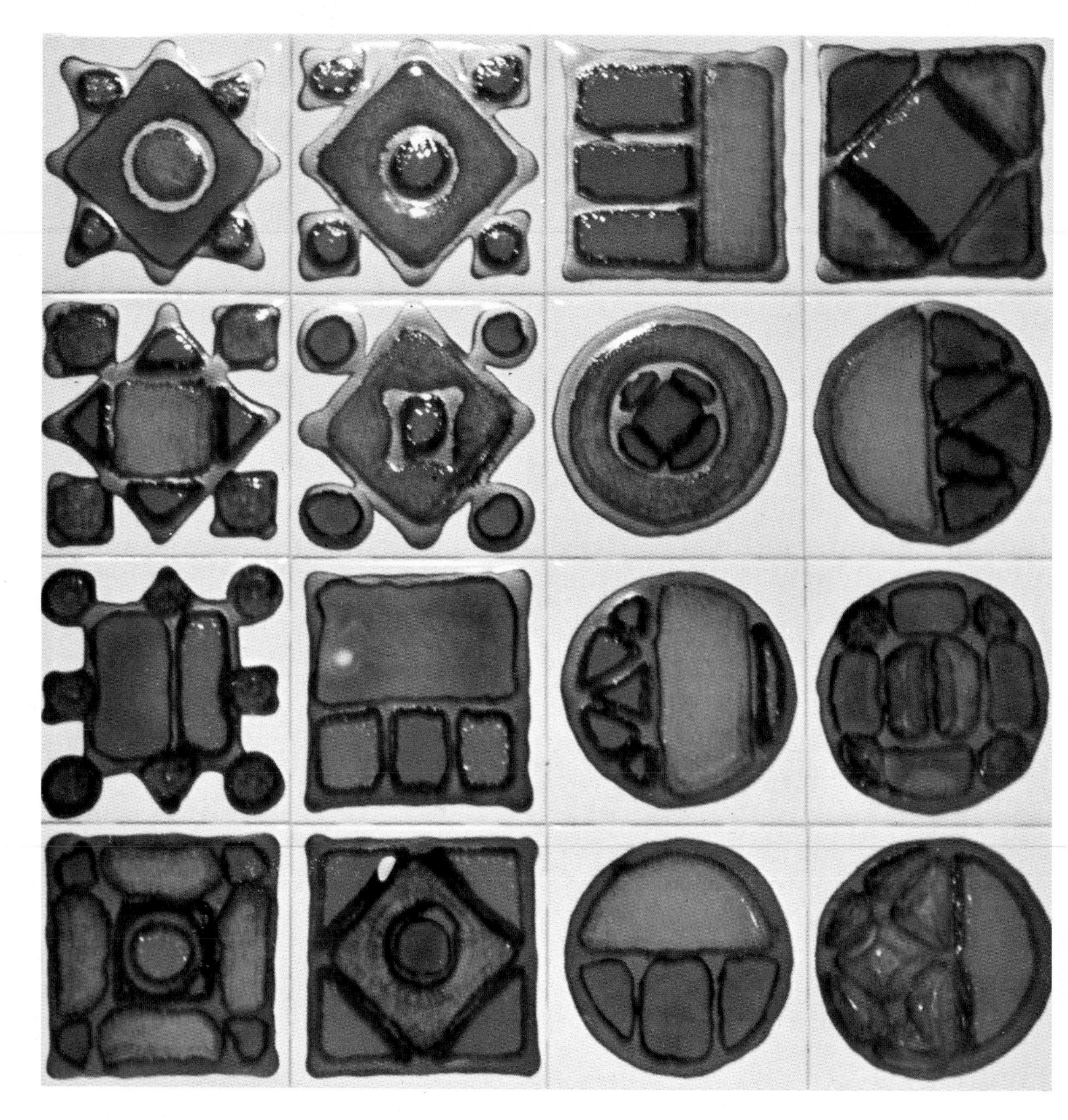

1 Trailed-glaze designs by The Kenneth Clark Pottery, London

Making and Decorating Pottery Tiles

by B. C. SOUTHWELL

WATSON-GUPTILL PUBLICATIONS
NEW YORK

*First published in the United States of America 1972 by Watson-Guptill Publications,
a division of Billboard Publications, Inc.,
165 West 46 Street, New York, N.Y.*

*First published 1972 in Great Britain by Faber and Faber Ltd.,
3 Queen Square, London WC1N 3AU*

Manufactured in England

First Printing, 1972

Library of Congress Cataloging in Publication Data

Southwell, B C
Making and decorating pottery tiles.

Bibliography: p.
1. Tiles. 2. Glazing (Ceramics). I. Title.
TP837.S65 738.6 72-3489
ISBN 0-8230-2988-3

Acknowledgements

I wish to express my gratitude for the help and co-operation I have received from the following: The Management and Staff of Candy Tiles Ltd., Devon; Mr. Tarquin Cole, Ceramic Consultants Ltd., London; Mr. D. Sellars, Milborne Port, Dorset; The Students of Loughborough College of Art; Mr. A. Griffith, Senior Lecturer in Ceramics; Mr. R. Rogers, Head of The Department of Three Dimensional Design; and Mr. E. Sharp, Principal of Loughborough College of Art.

I should like to express special thanks to Mr. Kenneth Clark who helped in fostering my original interest in making and decorating tiles.

Conversion Formula

Centigrade to Fahrenheit

example: $100° C \times \frac{9}{5} = 180 \quad 180 + 32 = 212° F$

Fahrenheit to Centigrade

example: $212° F - 32 = 180 \quad 180 \times \frac{5}{9} = 100° C$

CONVERSION TABLE

Centigrade	*Fahrenheit*
10°	50°
20°	68°
50°	132°
100°	212°
150°	300°
200°	392°
250°	482°
300°	572°
350°	662°
400°	752°
450°	810°
500°	932°
550°	1022°
600°	1112°
650°	1202°
700°	1292°
750°	1382°
800°	1472°
850°	1562°
900°	1652°
950°	1742°
1000°	1832°
1050°	1922°
1100°	2012°
1150°	2102°
1200°	2192°
1250°	2282°
1300°	2372°

Contents

Geometrical design, coloured inlayed clay. Author's collection

Illustrations

Relief tile with coloured sand surface. Sand applied to wet clay. Fired at stoneware temperature. Designed and made by a student at Loughborough College

COLOUR PLATES

TEXT FIGURES

All photographs and drawings by the author unless otherwise stated

Fig. 1. Instanbul, Mosque of Rüstem Pasha, pilaster with tiles

1 · An Introduction to Tiles

Tiles have been made almost throughout the history of ceramics. In recent years the popularity of the tile has increased to the point where a single decorated tile is an acceptable gift.

The present range of commercially made tiles, both plain and decorated, is immense and the potential that tiles possess, as a medium for artistic expression, is fully realized by artist potters working in small studios.

The tile is easy to make, its flat surface inviting innumerable ceramic decorating techniques and, in addition, its simplicity of form lends confidence to the designer when decorative treatment is being applied.

The individual potter working in isolation may not be fully aware of the tile capabilities, but by seeing historical examples of tile work, a wider understanding of what can be achieved may be gained—together with the stimulation that comes through seeing other people's work.

There are, however, pitfalls to historical reference: believing that what history shows us is the best solution to a problem is perhaps the major misconception that arises. Tradition should always be questioned and not blindly accepted; this applies equally to both aesthetic and technical judgements. To clarify this point, examine the pressures applied on designers in any one period. It will be found that social, economic and fashionable ideas will, to varying extents, have had a direct influence on the work. Compare the results of this enquiry with the requirements we are ourselves imposing and the outcome may be tilework with a similar content to that of any one historical period, but it should never be an exact copy that results from blind acceptance of tradition. The purpose behind making and decorating tiles must be apparent to their maker and only when this information is present can the history of tiles be used as a constructive and instructive element within one's own design standards.

Examples of historical tilework are innumerable and difficulty may be found in deciding where to start one's enquiries.

The most elaborate tiles are undoubtedly those found in Middle-Eastern cultures. These are of an unbelievable richness and used on an architectural scale and in a setting not found elsewhere in the world. In the same way as western gothic cathedrals are encrusted with carved stone ornament, Middle-Eastern mosques are often covered from foundation to roof with brilliantly coloured tiles.

Less elaborate in use, but no less interesting, are those tiles produced in European countries. These often give a social document on the period in which they were made, describing the dress, customs and technology of the period in graphic form. There does not seem to be a subject that the tile maker has not at some time used for decoration, or a ceramic technique that has not been used by the tile designer to gain the required result.

Design styles and ceramic techniques are linked in the mind with the cultures that have made greatest use of them. In this way most people associate painted tiles with the Dutch; inlayed coloured clay with the English; and brilliantly coloured, complex designs with the Middle-Eastern countries. This immediate association is only part of the truth. It will be found on investigation that many other qualities and styles were used by different cultures other than those to which most acclaim has been given.

Fig. 2. Dutch tile (author's collection)

The very simple yet versatile shapes that a tile may take, possibly account for the diversity of response in the designer's mind. One may look on tiles as performing the same service to the broad field of ceramics as the invention of paper performed to the graphic arts. They do this by representing an easily made and immediately accessible surface upon which to work.

Due to the complexity of material available for reference in the world-wide scene of ceramics, it may be found desirable, in order to simplify our initial investigations, to concentrate on readily accessible examples. Historical examples of particular interest are early church buildings and nineteenth-century and early twentieth-century domestic and municipal buildings, where an extremely varied selection of tilework may be found, and its function and effectiveness of the decoration all the more apparent for being seen *in situ.*

These nineteenth- and twentieth-century examples are quite common and may be seen in such places as the front porches of 'Victorian' villas, where the floor and side walls are used as focal points for highly decorated tilework, as well as being a good protection against the weather. There are also many examples of Victorian commemorative plaques made in terracotta, often linked to the architecture by decorative bands of tilework running at intervals along the brickwork.

Shops may be found to supply interesting examples of tilework, ranging from the modern style of decorative façade to the basically hygienic use of tiles in butchers' or fishmongers' shops, which often show animals and related subject-matter painted on large tile panels. This type of work is now becoming less frequently seen due to the demolition of old property. In some towns the street names are spelt out in inlaid clay tiles and some old public conveniences have entertaining tilework.

The mass of nineteenth-century architecture seems to take on the same overall pattern, but if one looks at the detailing it will be found to be extremely varied in its design motifs. This variation was carried on to the internal fitments of buildings; such things as fireplaces in Victorian houses will be found to contain what seems like a never-ending supply of new designs: the iron fireplaces may be the same but their tile insets are invariably different and it is most unusual to find the same designs used from house to house or from room to room in any one terraced block of villas.

The techniques used to make nineteenth-century tiles are as varied as their design content. Inlaying, copperplate engraved transfers, under- and over-glaze painting, impressed and relief modelling with coloured glazes, were all used to

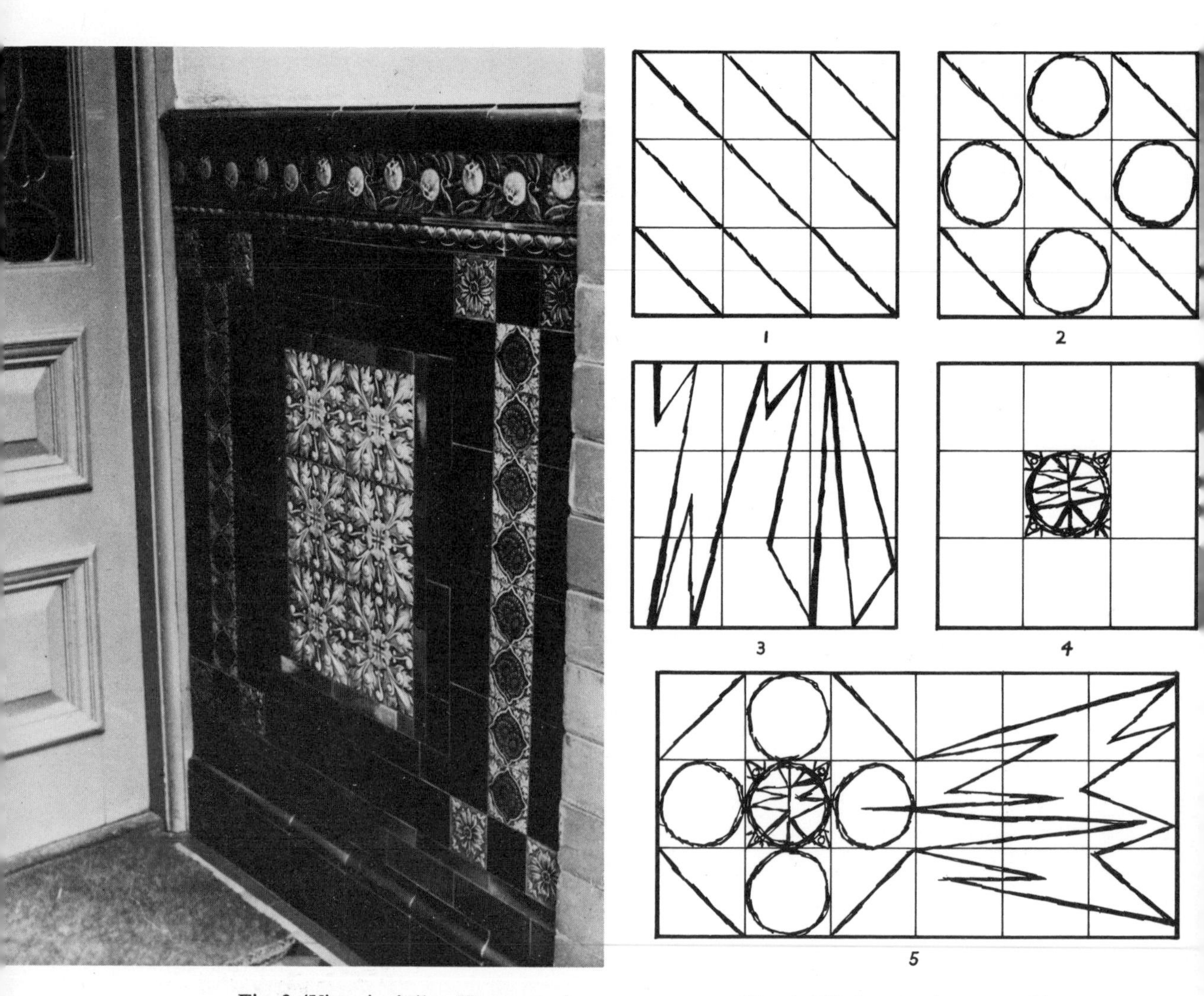

Fig. 3. 'Victorian' tiles. House porch

Fig. 4. Tile formats (see page 19)

enlarge the choice of designs. Many of these techniques have now been dropped from factory practice due to their expense or slowness in production and it is now being left to the individual artist potter to fill the design gap and increase the qualities possible in tile decoration.

The diversity of historical tile designs can often be, on first sight, an inhibiting factor for anyone wishing to create their own tilework. The figurative elements in historical tilework can often obscure the underlying design values. These values are the most important factor for the creative designer; it is not the style or figurative content that should take predominant place when looking at historical tiles as reference points. It is the constructional elements that should be analysed, giving as they do the greatest stimulation and confidence in one's own work. If a tile exists as a single unit, the design values are those related to its surface and physical boundaries. If, on the other hand, a tile's design is only part of many other tiles, notice must be taken first of the total scheme and then of the individual tile's contribution.

Placing one tile next to another creates many complex problems and often unforeseen results. The most obvious complication that multi-tile designs create, is the grid pattern set up by the joints between each tile. In most designs the grid pattern should be one's first consideration: is it to be utilized as a design factor or ignored? If one is to ignore the grid set up by the tile joints, greater freedom of expression (as is found in painting on canvas) may be achieved. Generally it will be found that most tilework fits one of the following formats (see fig. 4).

1. Single-tile repeat, following grid pattern.
2. Repetition of two or more tiles, following grid pattern.
3. Freely composed design ignoring grid pattern.
4. Single tile existing alone.
5. Any combination of above.

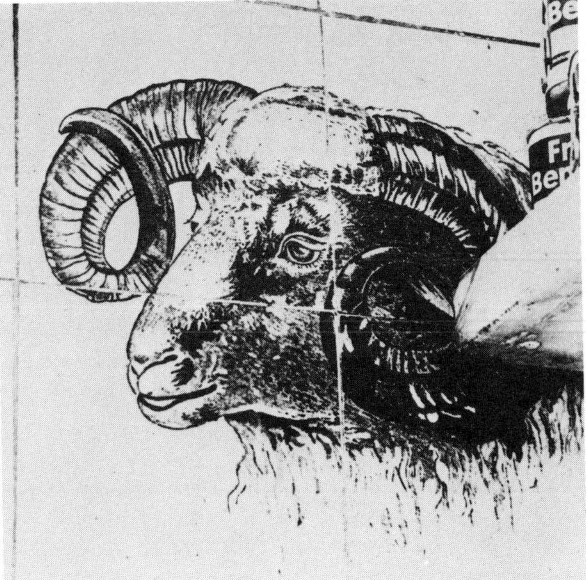

Fig. 5. Tiles on a butcher's shop

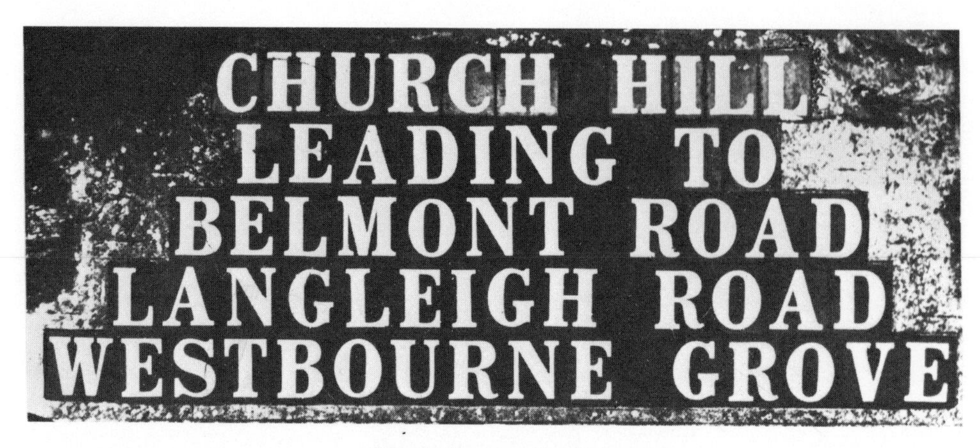

Fig. 6. Street name tiles

The repetition of a single-tile design is one of the most obvious and frequently used principles, but it does create many problems. Historical reference can show some of these problems and the ways in which they have been solved. Most tiles will work very well as plain simple shapes cladding a surface or structure; this is their usual basic utility over which may be laid other requirements, such as colour, shape and decoration. The outcome of these requirements always depends on the individual designer's tastes and attitudes but they should, together with the tiles' basic utility, fit the overall environment in which the tile will eventually exist. There are no universal rules to apply to design problems; only those rules discovered and applied in any given situation. One useful method of solving design problems is to view the work from its technical aspects, and although technical skill will never give the complete answer to design problems, it will enable a direction to be taken that may prove fruitful in allowing the creative imagination to develop.

In some ways it is the *raison d'être* of this book to break down, and make familiar, tile-making techniques so that the designer is less inhibited by the purely technical aspects of the craft thereby leaving him free to work in a more creative manner.

Fig. 7. 'Victorian' fireplace tiles

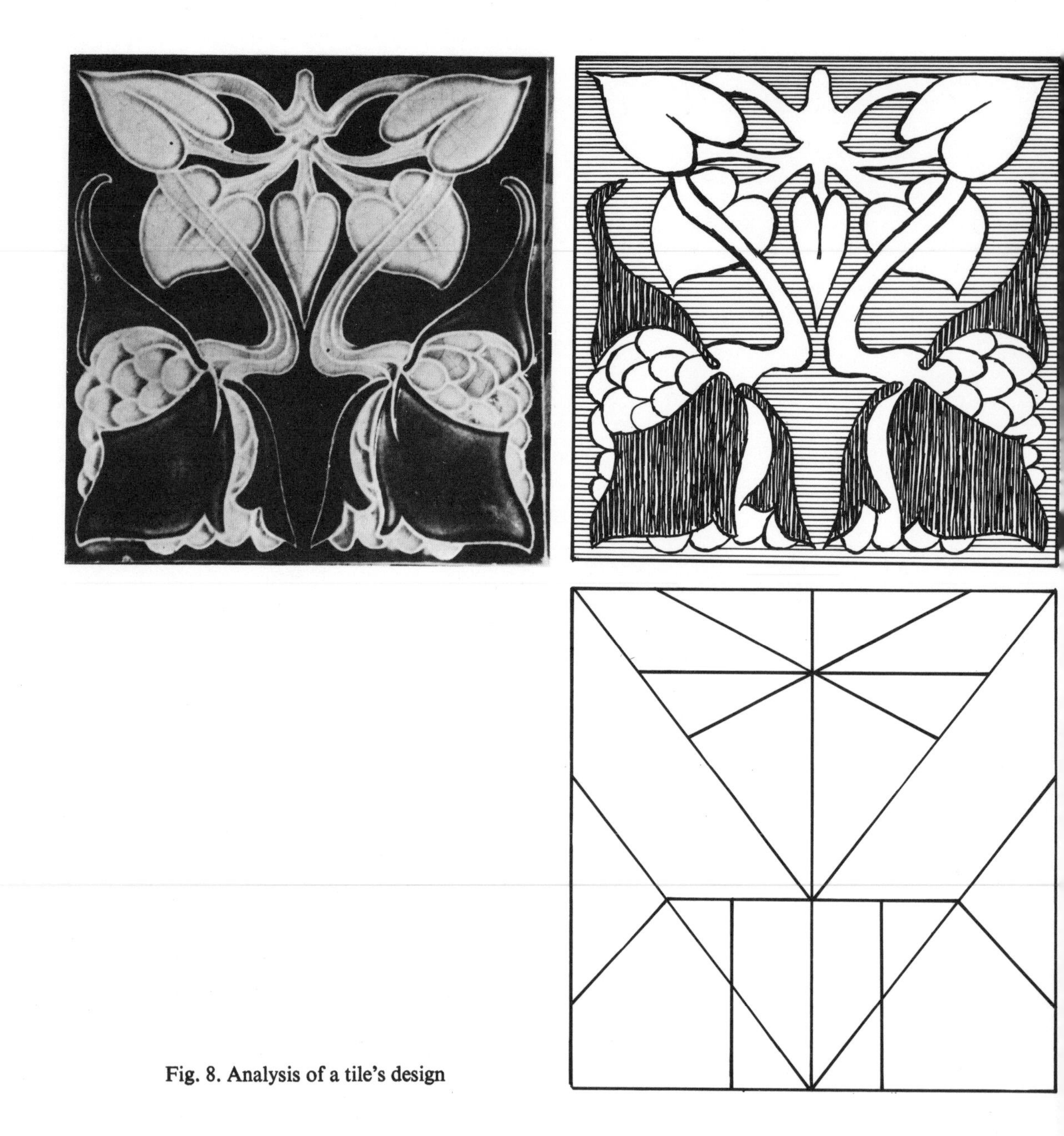

Fig. 8. Analysis of a tile's design

2 · Handmade Tiles

Under certain conditions the handmade tile can be a troublesome thing to make. The main problem is the need to dry the clay slowly and evenly and so avoid warpage. Clays of open texture, those containing sand or grog, are best for tilemaking. Such clay may be purchased, or the sand and grog may be added to an existing smooth clay. The following points must be observed when adding sand or grog to clay:

1. Prepare enough clay for the completion of all the tiles to be made. This will give all the tiles similar properties in drying, shrinking and firing.
2. Weigh the materials, sand or grog and clay. Record the proportions in which they are mixed. This note-taking procedure is the rule in all pottery technique as it presents recorded experience and is helpful to understanding how ceramic materials work.
3. Wet the sand or grog—AFTER weighing and before adding to clay. If the sand or grog is added dry, difficulty will be found in producing an even mixture and moisture will be taken from the clay, making it lose its plasticity.
4. Do not add too much sand or grog; this contributes to the loss of plasticity. The correct amount varies from clay to clay. Tests can be made with a handful of clay; adding sand or grog until a roll of the clay breaks easily when bent. When this happens, too much sand or grog has been used and so we may assume that a little less will give the correct amount. If difficulty is found or anticipated, the suppliers of the clay will give suggestions on the correct proportions.
5. After adding all the sand or grog to the amount of clay needed to make all the tiles, knead and wedge more thoroughly than in normal clay preparation. This should ensure a complete mix..

At this point it should be remembered that if a gritty surface is an interference with any proposed decoration, smooth, ungrogged clay should be used. Extra precaution in the preparation and drying of smooth clay tiles is necessary.

'Sliced-block' method for making the basic tile unit

1. Take enough clay to make all tiles needed. If many tiles are required, say 24 or more, divide the clay into smaller lumps that would produce 6 to 9 tiles, according to size and thickness, and be easy to handle. The average workable size of tile would be 6 in. sq. and up to ½ in. thick, this depending on the individual's preference and the type of design to be carried out. Remember that the average thickness of a handmade tile is such that it is difficult to detect air pockets or flaws in the consistency of the clay. These air pockets and flaws may cause irrepairable damage when the tiles are drying and being fired. The clay lumps should therefore be wedged once more before cutting into slices.
2. After wedging, the clay is knocked into a regular cubic shape. The size of this shape depends upon the dimensions of the proposed tile. If the tile is to be 6 in. square and ½ in. thick, then the clay shape should be 6–8 in. wide and deep, and as high as allows 6–9 tiles to be made at one time. There should always be an excess in the shape of clay from which the tiles are cut; this allows trimming at a later stage.
3. The block of clay is now placed firmly on a flat board or tabletop, so that it sticks to the surface and does not move when sliced into tiles. The following tools will be needed to do the slicing:

   Two pieces of wood, 12–15 in. long and approximately 1 in. square. These 'woods' should have sawcuts in them, running parallel across one face of their width. The space between cuts should equal the thickness of the tile to be made. By using two opposite sides of the 'woods' it is possible to have various widths between sawcuts and so give choice as to thickness of tile. If these extra, differently spaced cuts are used, care must be taken that the sides match when cutting tiles.

   You will also need a length of strong thin wire or nylon thread. Two pieces of dowelling approximately 1 in. long should be tied one to each end of the wire. The wire should exceed the width of the tile to be made by at least 4 in.
4. The 'woods' are now held, one in each hand, with matching sawcuts at the bottom, near the tabletop and facing towards oneself. The wire is placed in the first sawcut from the bottom of the 'woods'. The dowels will help in retaining the wire in this position and with reference to Fig. 9 and practice,

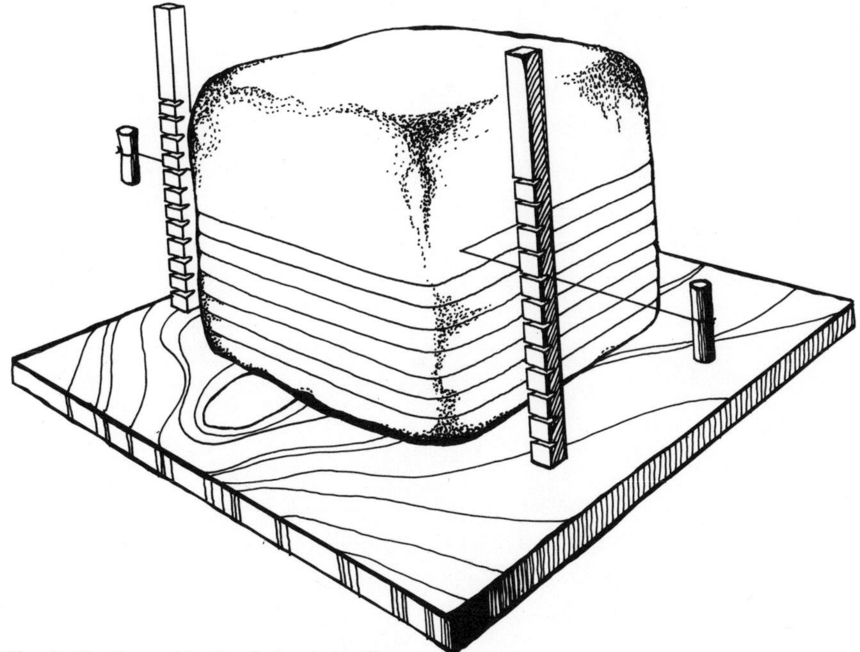

Fig. 9. Cutting a block of clay into tiles

the easiest way of holding 'woods' and wires will be found.

The hands, 'woods' and wire are now placed behind the block of clay. By pulling outward with both hands, the wire is made taut.

Whilst pressing the ends of the 'woods' firmly down on the tabletop, the wire, 'woods' and hands are drawn back towards the body and the wire cuts through the clay block. This movement is repeated, with the wire in the next sawcut up, for each cut. The result from this repeated action is a pile of clay slices which are the thickness of the tiles being made.

5. The slices of clay are now carefully separated and laid flat on a board. The slices of clay should now be left until leather-hard, before any trimming is done. The slices should be turned over from time to time to allow the clay to dry evenly. Care should be taken that the clay slices do not lay in a draught of air which is likely to dry the edges before the centre, resulting in warpage.
6. When leather-hard, each slice is trimmed to the shape of the desired tile. If, however, some surface decoration is to be applied, it should be done before trimming, as any work on a trimmed tile tends to distort its shape. There

will, of course, be times when decoration of a trimmed tile is necessary and care should then be taken to minimize the interference to the shape of the tile. To produce accurately shaped tiles of the same size, it is necessary to use a template when trimming, and a narrow-bladed knife. The template may be made from hardboard or wood and it should have a reasonably large-sized handle with which to hold it steady whilst cutting the clay. If complex

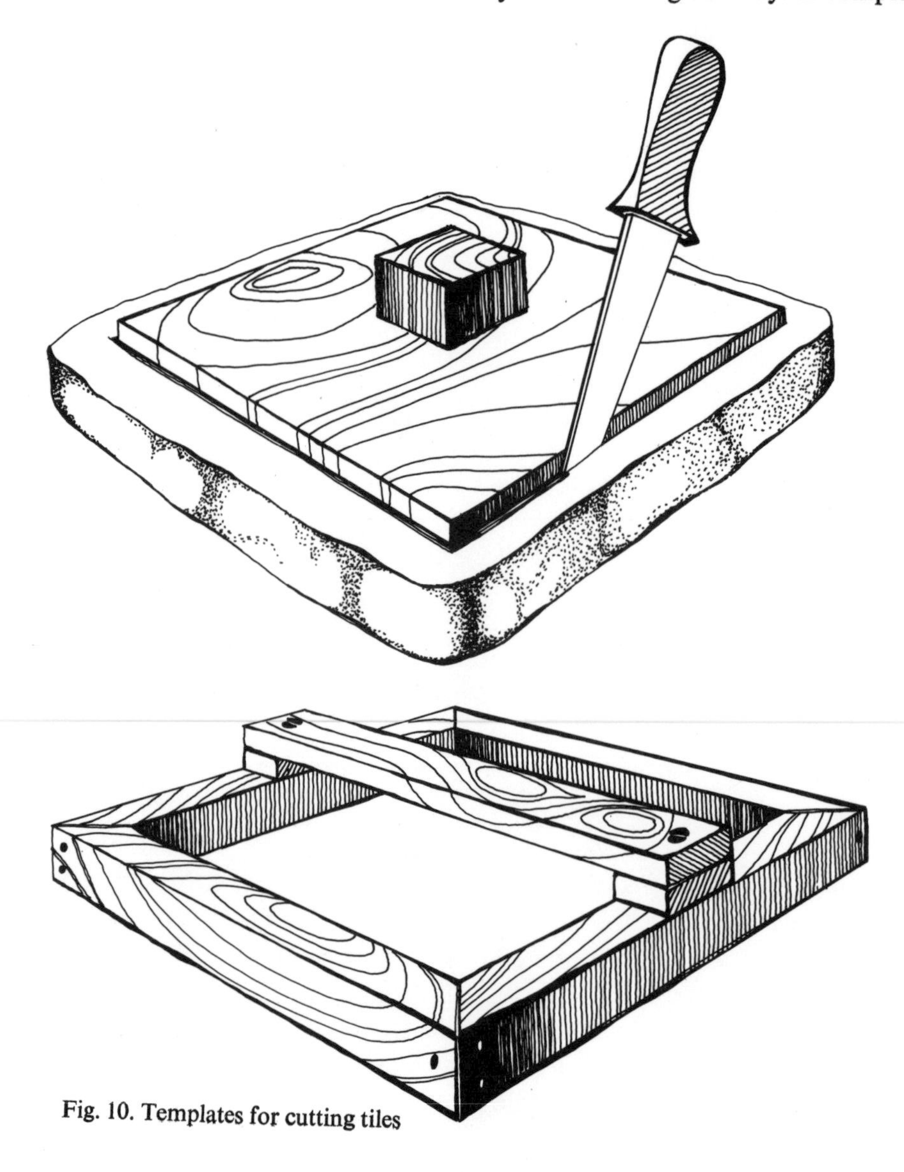

Fig. 10. Templates for cutting tiles

or free-shape tiles are being made, then cardboard or even paper templates may be used, as these materials are more readily cut to shape than hardboard or wood.

7. After the tiles are trimmed to size they are ready for further drying.

If the tiles are plain or have only slight surface decoration, they may be dried by standing on edge. The first tile being supported by a lump of hard clay or a block of wood. Each subsequent tile is then supported away from the preceding one, by two small pellets of clay, placed one in each of the top corners of the tile. This creates a gap between the tiles as they stand and allows air to circulate allowing the tile to dry evenly back and front. If there is any irregularity in the tiles' shape, which prevents them from being stacked in this manner, they may be dried evenly by being laid on racking made from slats of wood (Fig. 11). Should any signs of warpage appear at this late

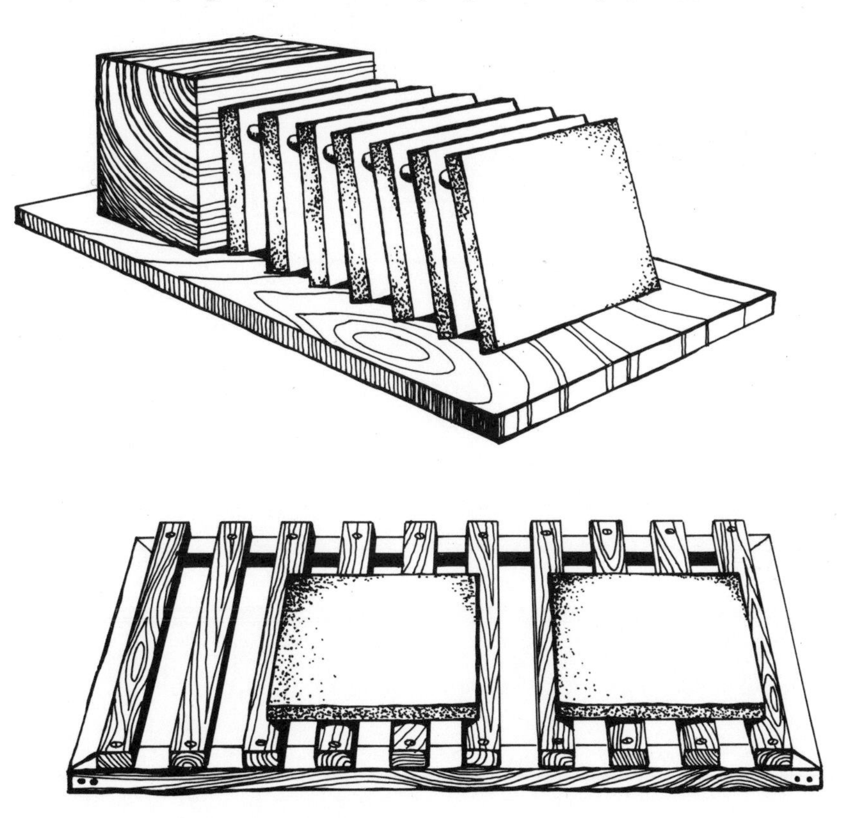

Fig. 11. Drying handmade tiles

stage, gentle but firm pressure may be applied to counteract the bending. If the tile is plain it should be laid on a flat surface, concave side down, and pressure applied to the centre and downwards.

Bending leather-hard tiles is likely to cause cracks in the clay, so great care must be taken, and if any doubts arise as to the success of the venture, it would be advisable to lay a damp cloth over the offending tile to soften the clay a little before bending out the warpage.

If the tile does not bend readily, do not force it, as there is a further chance of correcting warpage when the tile is fired. When the tile is packed into the kiln, it should be placed in such a way as to put its weight on the warped area. This is not a guaranteed answer to the problem, but only one to be used if bending at the leather-hard stage fails.

Decorating handmade tiles

Slicing a block of clay is the most direct method of making tiles. It is my intention to cover, in the following description, equally direct methods of decorating such tiles. Relief modelling, surface texturing, incised, inlayed and trailed or painted slipwork are some methods that deal directly with the wet-clay tile.

RELIEF MODELLING ON WET-CLAY TILES

The basic technical requirement for relief modelling is that the base clay tile and the clay modelled on its surface should be of the same consistency. If the design is such that it has to be made from fully plastic clay, then the work should be carried out on the newly sliced clay, without any drying taking place. Should stiff or leather-hard clay be used for decoration, then it must be used when the tile is at the same state in drying.

Tiles with relief modelling are invariably used as wall surfaces or decorative panels. They are not suitable for tabletops or similar working surfaces. In designing a relief tile we have then to consider the finished work's position, which is normally a vertical one. Under most circumstances the lighting of vertical work is from above, daylight or artificial. This fact is important, as we find the major influencing factor in relief work is tone. Tiles used on walls and hanging panels are there to entertain the eye and enhance the environment.

This must be kept in mind, together with the fact that we are dealing in terms of tone, so that a stimulating tonal arrangement may be made. Colour, line, etc., also play their part, but as the initial work is monochrome, the tone is all important.

An experiment in tone may be made by taking a clay tile, cutting various shapes from its surface, also applying various shapes to its surface. Next, move the tile so that a strong light falls on it from different directions. Note how the emphasis on one form changes to another when the tile is moved. A further experiment in tone would be to incise lines across the surface of a clay tile and parallel to another. Start with a very faint incision and increase the depth of each successive line. You will find when this is done that the tone of the lines becomes darker, the deeper they are. This may seem a very simple fact, something that should be obvious to anyone, but it is the foundation for the subtle variations in tone that will enhance relief work.

Other qualities of light are added to the work when it is glazed. If the glaze is matt in surface, a softening effect takes place, but if a high-gloss glaze is used, many unexpected things may occur, the most obvious of these being the addition of strongly reflected light in small patches. Reflections may enhance a relief design, but more usually they tend to interrupt and confuse the modelled form.

The colours in which the relief are finished may also upset the relationships existing in the modelled form. A general rule for colouring is, that if any part of the modelling is meant to be dark in tone, that part should have a dark colour applied to it. If one applies light colours to the dark-tone areas, the modelled form will be lightened and the work may be visually confusing.

Methods by which clay may be modelled on to the surface of a tile are numerous and often become the signature of the artist. Direct modelling is perhaps the most obvious; that is by building upwards from the clay surface with small pieces of clay, merging one into another. An alternative to this would be the prefabrication of clay shapes, made away from the tile's surface, to be stuck on to the tile on completion (Fig. 12). The choice of technique should always be made in relation to the type of design to be carried out.

SURFACE TEXTURING

Surface texturing has endless possibilities. The textures may be made by impressions in the clay, by the addition of clay to the tile's surface, or by the

Fig. 12. Prefabricated clay shapes

combination of these two techniques. Anything, provided it is harder than the clay, may be pressed into the tile's surface to give pattern or texture: nuts and bolts, stiff leaves from plants, cut plaster shapes (Fig. 13), anything that results in a stimulating quality in clay. What is important, is the use to which these tools are put. Once again experiment is important; collect a number of items which you feel could give interesting impressions, use them singly, together or in some simple repetitive fashion. Any tiles resulting from these experiments may be kept for reference, and further use may be made of them as vehicles for glaze experiments. Remember that surface texturing may be used as an end in itself, or it may be used to enrich bigger, bolder modelled relief forms.

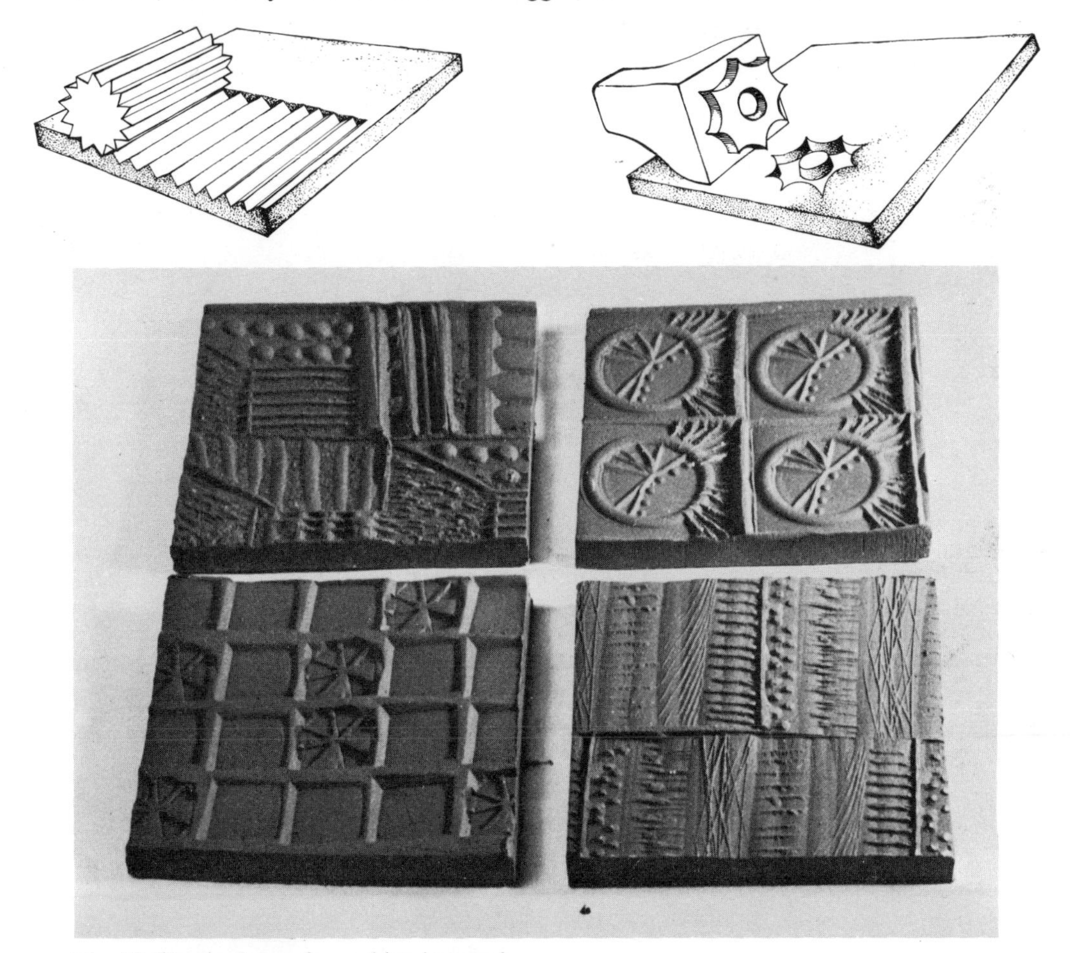

Fig. 13. Plaster shapes for making impressions

INCISED DECORATION

Incised work is, as the word suggests, simply cutting into the surface with line, as one would draw with pencil on paper. Sgraffito can be considered as incised decoration. This is a traditional technique with many possibilities for those who enjoy draughtsmanship. After the tiles are sliced and separated from the block of clay, one surface is covered in a contrasting coloured slip. The tile is then left until leather-hard and trimmed. It is now possible to cut through the layer of coloured slip to reveal the contrasting colour of the clay tile underneath. Designs made this way may be in line, area or texture and richness may be added using coloured slips painted on the surface in various areas or by the application of coloured glazes when the tile has been fired.

INLAYING

Areas of the tile's surface are cut away to an approximate one-eighth in depth. These areas are then filled, either with a different coloured plastic clay or a slip. This is done when the tile has reached its leather-hard stage. The tile is then left to dry further, but not completely, and the excess clay or slip is trimmed off by scraping around the inlayed design. This technique is suitable for producing line, area and textures.

TRAILED AND PAINTED SLIPWORK

Slip trailing and painting is a very popular traditional pottery technique. I do not intend to describe it further, as information on the subject may be had from almost any other book on ceramics. However, I would like to say that richness may be added to this technique by the application of coloured glazes or by underglaze colourwork done, before glazing and after the biscuit firing, on the initial design.

FREE-FORM TILES

Free-form tiles present problems peculiar to their shape. They may be treated with the techniques already mentioned, but the choice of shape and size of the tiles must be carefully considered.

2 Hand-painted tile; outline executed in underglaze colours and coloured areas painted in glazes

If the tiles are to fit together after firing, they must be cut into shapes that do not have any peculiarities in drying. Some examples of this will be easily understood, for instance in the case of a long thin triangular tile. In this shape the pointed end of the triangle will dry more rapidly than the wider base, and in doing so may promote warpage. If it should be necessary to have an area of tile such as this, it would be wise to cut the tile into two or three pieces, across its length. This will give us pieces which are more constant in their drying behaviour. Other shapes cause different drying problems; some of these are given in diagram form (Fig. 14).

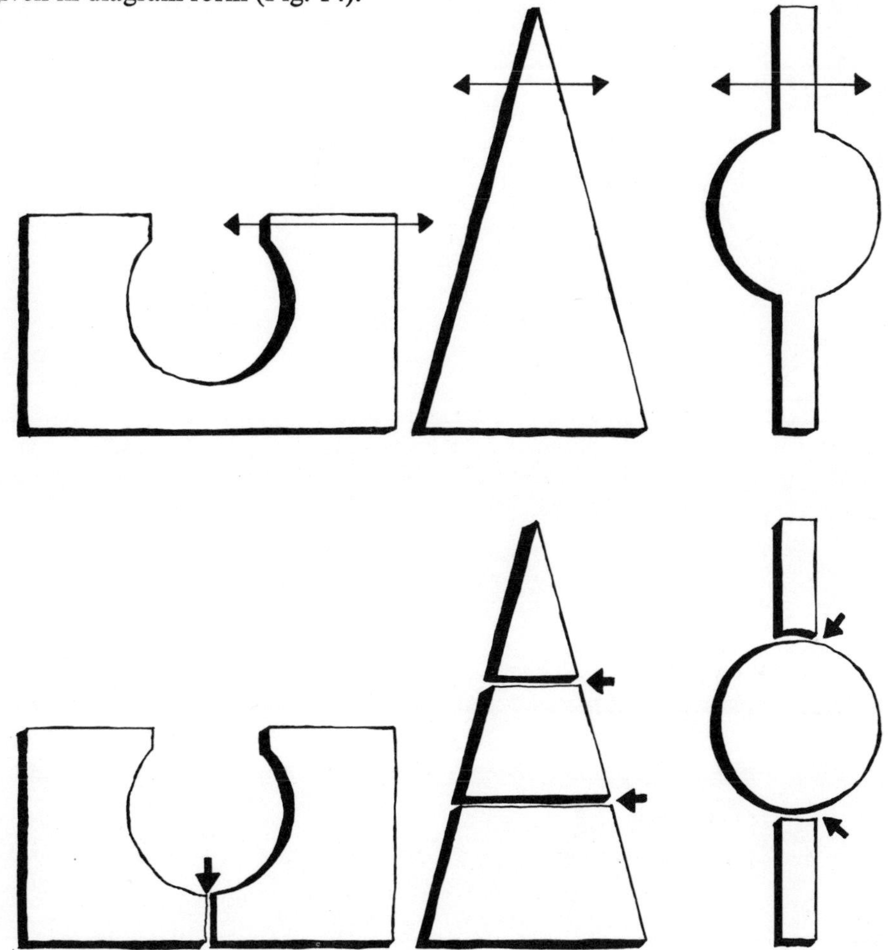

Fig. 14. Prevention of warpage in free-shaped tiles

Fig. 15. Tiles as component shapes

The designs made from free-form tiles should be worked out prior to commencing the actual claywork. This is because the complexity of shapes that may be involved will be more difficult to handle than that found in regularly shaped tiles. Cutting paper or card into the desired shapes is the most direct way of observing how the design is to be made.

The shaped tiles may be handled in various ways. Stained-glass windows illustrate one method of fitting free-shaped tiles into a design. If this idea is used, the gaps between the tiles may either be ignored or integrated into the design (Fig. 15). This statement applies to all tilework but in freely shaped tiles the lines formed by the edges of the tiles are more predominant than those formed by regular tiles. Another method of using free-shaped tiles is to break the design down into its component shapes and use these shapes as each tile (Fig. 16). If it is found that certain components are not easily made as a single tile, they should be split into two or more pieces.

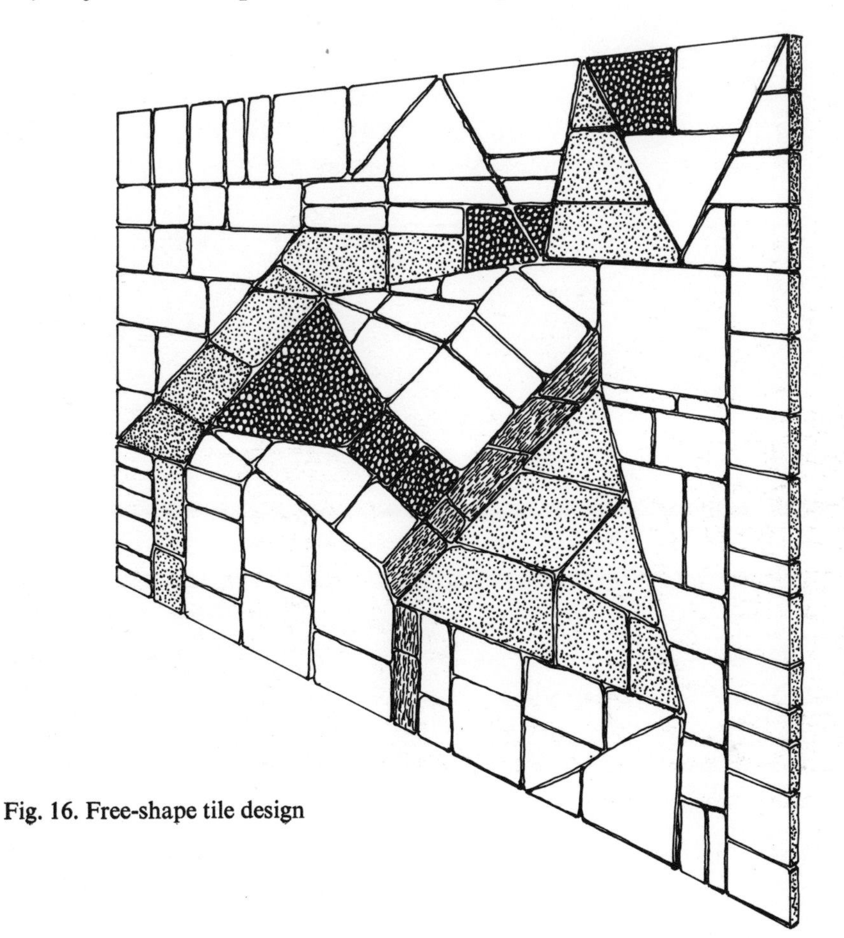

Fig. 16. Free-shape tile design

The area which free-shaped tiles cover may have, if it is desired, a freely shaped edge. When mounted for display they may be presented in such a way as to preserve this edge as a dominant design factor, or they may be set into some regular shape, made from tiles or stuck on a background of some other material.

When creating a design with or on tiles, always make a study of how the clay, either plastic or leather-hard, behaves under various conditions. I have already stressed the necessity of experiment. If knowledge and understanding of the properties of clay are to be enlarged, detailed inspection and speculation are needed whilst experimenting or working on an actual design.

Clay is a most responsive material and the effects that occur when working it are innumerable. Even at the early stage of cutting the clay block into slices, things happen to the clay surface which may be desirable in any particular design. One instance of this is when two wires are twisted together and used for cutting. The resulting clay surface is a highly decorative fluted design, which may be varied with the direction of each cut made through the clay.

It must also be remembered that qualities gained easily in this responsive material are as easily destroyed through clumsy handling. It is therefore very necessary to give consideration to the layout of materials and tools when working on clay tiles. Some of the following points may help towards efficient work:

1. Do not allow the hands to become encrusted with clay. This clay will dry off rapidly and fall on to the soft clay surface of the tiles, often causing damage to subtly modelled surfaces.
2. For the same reason tools should be kept clean from drying clay.
3. Try to work the design on an inclined surface, with the light facing towards or to one side of oneself. This will be as near to the work's final vertical position as is possible.
4. Make sure that dry lumps of clay are kept apart from plastic clay used for modelling.
5. Have near to hand a comprehensive selection of tools. This would include useful implements other than those recognized as pottery tools; such things as Surform blades, hacksaw blades—rough and fine—and odd pieces of wood or metal. These can often give shapes that would be awkward to obtain by conventional tools. In fact, almost anything of a handleable size may be useful at some time or other.

'Aquarium' design made in earthenware, with pooled glazes in the details. Designed and made by a student at Loughborough College of Art

An example of the interest that may be created in a design by using both negative and positive prints. Note how by changing the tonal arrangement of a design, the weight and focal points of the pattern are altered (*By courtesy of Mr. D. Sellars*)

3 · Cast and Moulded Tiles

Cast and moulded tiles have the advantage over handmade tiles that one design may be faithfully reproduced many times. Their disadvantage is that they need a great deal of preparatory work, involving materials other than clay, for the production of moulds and dies.

The following list of qualities will help in deciding which manufacturing technique to employ.

Handmade tiles

Average to heavy in finished weight.
May give versatile and complex designs.
Single or repeated motifs.
Modifications possible up to biscuit firing.
No other skills necessary than those for claywork.
Size limit usual in small studios approximately 1 ft. sq.

Slipcast tiles

Very light to heavy in finished weight.
Hollow or solid.
Accurate repetition of design.
Not normally modified after manufacture but experiments in modification can prove rewarding.
Skill with plaster needed to make moulds.
Clay needs special preparation to make casting-slip.
Design limitations unless elaborate moulds are made.
Size limit in small studios approximately 1 ft. 6 in. sq.

Pressmould tiles

Average to heavy in finished weight.
Hollow or solid.
Reasonably accurate repetition of design.
May be modified up to biscuit firing.
Other qualities same as for slipcasting.

Sandcast tiles

Average to heavy in finished weight.
Design limitations imposed by sand.
Exact repetition not possible.
Always solid.
Surface textured by sand which is major quality.

Extruded tiles

Average to heavy in finished weight.
Hollow or solid.
Exact repetition or variation of a single design.
Modification possible and extremely useful.
Pugmill or wad box required.
Skill needed to cut die or template.
Size limited in width, by the extrusion hole of pugmill or wad box, but length is variable.

Slipcasting tiles

MAKING THE MOULD

A model is made of the designed tile. It may be made from any material that is easily separated from a plastercast. The usual materials for model-making are clay, plaster or plasticine. Each of these three materials has its own special requirements when being used to make the model from which a cast is to be taken. Clay needs care in casting to avoid damage to its soft surface. Due to the softness of clay and plasticine it is difficult to obtain strict accuracy, but the surface of the latter is less prone to damage when a plaster cast is taken. Plaster models can give accuracy and there is no fear of damage when casting. They do, however, need special attention if they are to be freed easily from the plaster cast.

The design and making of the model must exclude all 'undercuts' (Fig. 17). If strict attention is not given to this point it will be difficult to remove clay and plasticine models from the cast, and impossible if the model is made from plaster. With clay and plasticine models small 'undercuts' will often be overlooked and the model may be successfully removed from the cast. When the first slipcast tile is taken from a mould made from a clay or plasticine model, very small 'undercuts' may cause damage. If this happens the offending area may be cut away from the mould and trial casts taken, until the problem is solved.

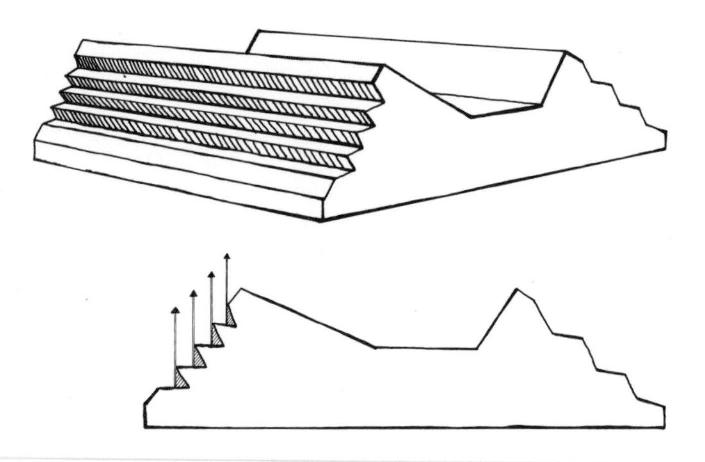

Fig. 17. Undercuts

Plaster models

A simple and direct method of making a plaster model is as follows:

1. Make a block of plaster which has the dimensions of the finished tile plus the amount that the clay, from which the tile will be made, shrinks when fired. Shrinkage may be calculated by firing a strip of clay of a fixed length and measuring before and after the firing. The difference between the length of the wet clay strip and its length when fired equals the amount, by proportion, that the plaster model will have to be made larger than the finished, fired tile.

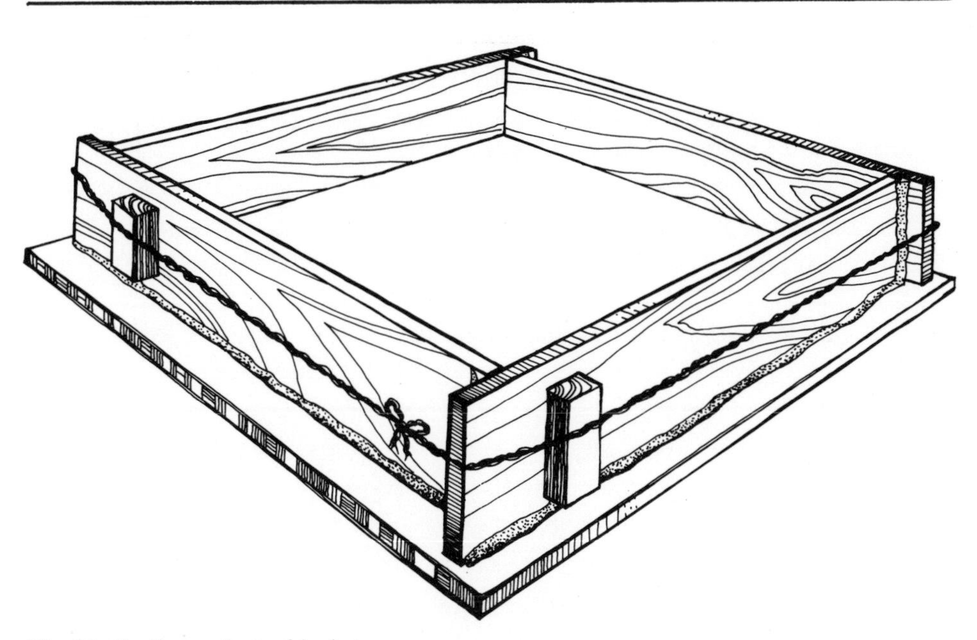

Fig. 18. Casting a plaster block

The plaster block is made by constructing the four side walls of a box from smooth pieces of wood (Fig. 18) which are held together with strong cord. The box is placed on the smooth, flat surface of a plate of glass or wooden board. The cracks around the bottom and corners of the box are sealed with strips of clay.

Plaster is poured into the box to a depth that exceeds the thickness of the finished model by approximately $\frac{1}{4}$ in. When the plaster is hard the box is removed.

2. The block of plaster is now made true to size and shape, using the smooth, flat surface given by the glass plate or wooden board as a true surface from which to measure. One edge of the block is worked true until it is at 90 deg. to the true bottom side. Each of the other three edges are now worked true to each other and to the bottom side. The top side should now be made flat and parallel to the bottom.
3. The four edges must now be made to slope inward from the bottom side of the model to the top side. The inward slope should be approximately $\frac{1}{16}$ in. out of the vertical, and it will allow the plaster model and subsequently the cast tiles to be removed easily from the mould.

All the above work may be carried out with a 'Surform' blade, a small plane or a strong sharp knife, cutting against the edge of a steel rule. A smooth finish may be added using a very fine 'wet and dry' abrasive paper.

4. The model is now ready to be cast as a blank tile or a design can be cut into its surface. If a design is cut into the plaster model, guard against 'undercuts'. When textures are used they should, as far as possible, be placed on the horizontal areas of the tile; if placed on vertical or sloping areas they may create 'undercuts' and cause the cast tile to stick to the mould. Any tool may be used to cut a design in a plaster model; lino-cutting tools, hacksaw blades, knives, chisels etc. will all give variety to the choice of design.
5. When the plaster model is complete its whole surface area must be sealed by sponging over with brown soft soap or 'Potters Size'. The soap should be allowed to soak into the plaster for a few minutes, then be wiped off with a clean, soft sponge. This process should be repeated several times, until the model's surface repels a light sprinkling of water. The soaping of a plaster model prevents the absorption, by the model, of water in the plaster used for making the mould.

MAKING THE MOULD

After removing any excess soap left on the surface of the model the mould-making process may commence.

1. Place the model on to the smooth surface previously used to make the rough plaster block. Seal the crack, around its base, with clay, wiping away excess clay with a clean, damp sponge. The clay seal prevents the plaster that is eventually poured over the model from running underneath, possibly displacing the model from its destined central position. A wooden box is now constructed around the model, similar to that used for making the rough block. A gap of approximately 1½ in. is left between the sides of the model and the wooden box. The height of the box should exceed the thickness of the model tile by at least 1½ in. The cracks at the base and corners of the box should be sealed with strips of clay and the whole construction fixed in some way that will resist any pressure put on it when the plaster is poured in (Fig. 18). Plaster is now poured over the model and into the box to a depth of at least 1½ in. above the highest point of the model. When all the plaster has been poured, the fingers should be lightly dabbled about over

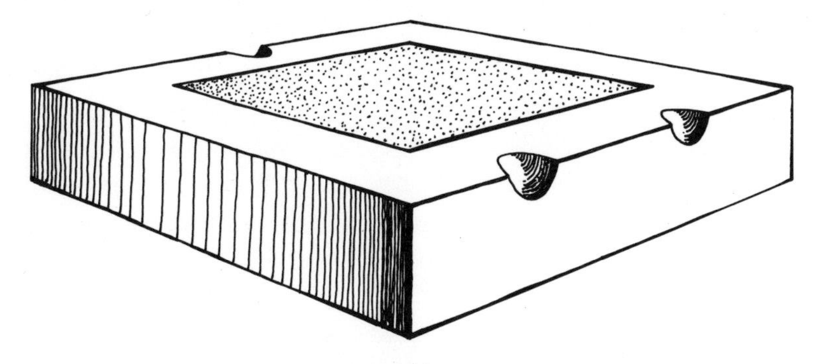

Fig. 19. Registration notches in a plaster mould

its surface to assist any air bubbles to rise, these may otherwise adhere to the model's surface, causing imperfections in the mould.

2. After the plaster has set hard, the box is removed and the top edges of the mould are trimmed even. The mould containing the model is now turned over. Cut three notches into the surface of the plaster surrounding the model, two notches on one side and one notch on the opposite side (Fig. 19). These notches will act as registration points for the other half of the mould now to be made.
3. Seal the back surface of the model and the surrounding surface of the mould with soft soap, remembering to wipe off any excess soap on the surface and ensure that enough time is allowed in soaping for the plaster's surface to resist a light sprinkling of water. Construct a wooden box around the mould and model. Each side of the box should be pressed firmly against the side of the plaster mould. The height of the box should exceed the depth of the mould by at least $1\frac{1}{2}$ in. (Fig. 20). Seal all cracks around the outside of the box with strips of clay. Pour in plaster and assist air bubbles to rise.

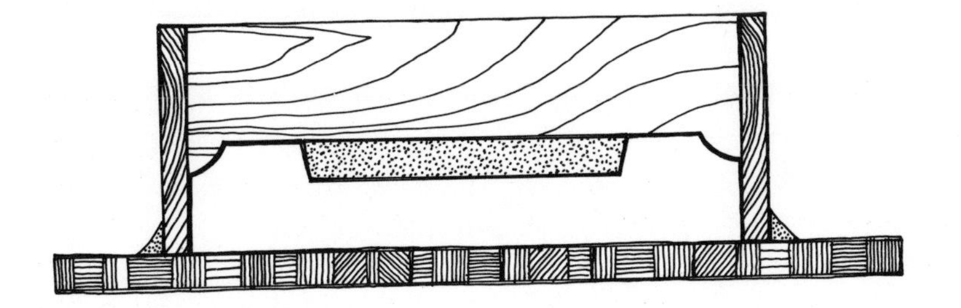

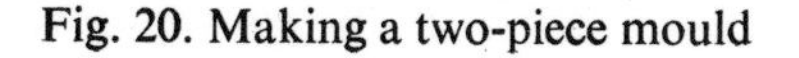

Fig. 20. Making a two-piece mould

4. After plaster has set, remove wooden box and trim all edges of plaster mould. Remove back part of mould (the last piece made). The model may now be removed from the front of the mould. This can often be a difficult thing to do, especially if the tile has a modelled on textured surface. If any trouble is encountered, the mould should be sharply tapped on back, front and sides. To avoid damage to the plaster's surface a piece of wood should be held over the point at which the mould is struck. If tapping the mould fails to release the model (some patience should be given to the task) it may be chipped out of the mould with a blunt chisel.
5. Two holes must now be cut through the back piece of the mould. These holes are to permit the mould to be filled with clay slip. They should be positioned in the corners of the tile, or, if the tile is freely shaped, at extreme points in its shape. The diameter of the holes at their narrowest point should be approximately 1 in. for hollow cast tiles and just over the maximum thickness of a solid cast tile (Fig. 21). After the holes are cut, the mould should be gently sponged all over its surface with clean water to remove any traces of soap or fragments of plaster. If any fine detail exists in the design, take care not to damage it whilst cleaning. The first cast may be taken from the mould after it has been allowed to dry completely.
6. The whole of the above procedure should be used when making moulds from clay or plasticine models. There is, however, no need to soap the model's surface. If clay is used for the model, do not pour plaster directly on to its surface, as this could wash away part of the design. Pour the plaster down the side of the wooden box and allow it to flow up and over the clay model.

   When dabbling one's fingers in the plaster to remove air bubbles, care must be taken not to disturb the soft surface of clay and plasticine models.

MIXING POTTERS PLASTER OR PLASTER OF PARIS

When making moulds for slipcasting or pressing, it is essential that all the moulds made should have the same properties of water absorption and casting properties. These properties are dependent on the amount of plaster added to any given quantity of water.

Proper mixing is also necessary if efficient moulding techniques are to be carried out, e.g. if a plaster model is made from a plaster mould, the plaster of the mould should be a 'stronger' mix than that plaster poured into it to

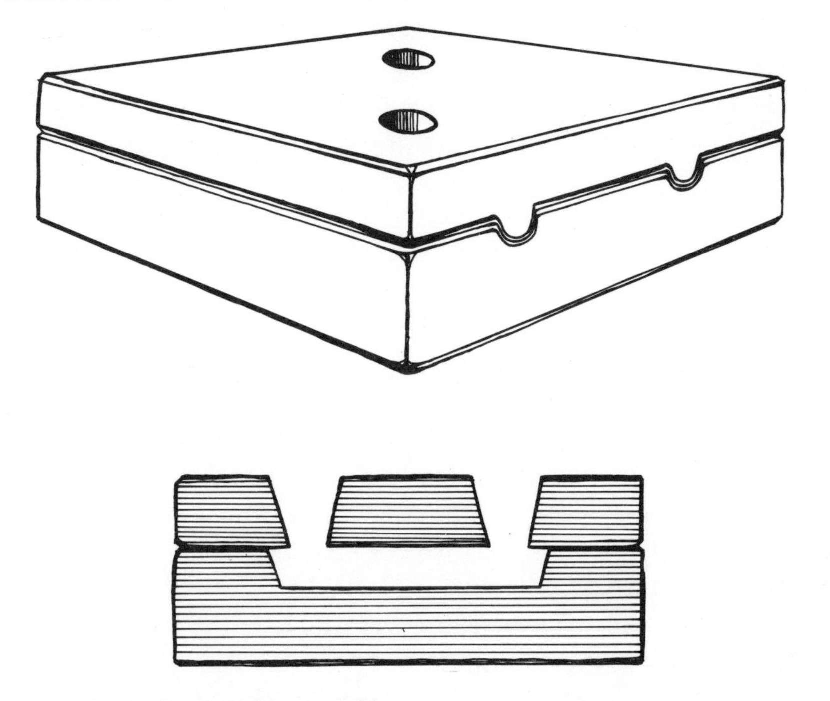

Fig. 21. 'Filling holes' in a mould

make the model. This is due to the fact that plaster expands when setting hard and if the mould is made from a 'weak' mix, the model may crack the mould.

An average mix for Potters Plaster would be—5 lb. plaster to 3 pints of water.

Potters Plaster takes a longer time to set hard than Plaster of Paris or Dental Plaster. This allows a thorough mix to be made and on no account should Potters Plaster be poured on to or into a cast until there are signs that it is thickening before setting hard. If Potters Plaster is poured too soon, it may separate out from the water and a soggy top surface will result.

If Plaster of Paris is used (Dental Plaster) less time is given before it sets hard; therefore greater speed is necessary.

As a general rule, Potters Plaster should always be used for making slipcast or pressing moulds. The reason for this is that Potters Plaster is coarser and has a greater capacity for the smooth and equal absorption of water from the clay used in casting or pressing.

Dental Plaster may be used for making models.

One general rule for studio practice that will prove useful is that plaster should be mixed in flexible plastic buckets. If any plaster remains in the bucket it should not be washed down a sink (this may block the drains) but should be left until hard, when it may be broken out of the bucket by bending the plastic. The solid waste plaster may then be thrown into a waste bin.

TAKING THE CAST

1. Tie the back and front pieces of the mould together with strong string, making sure that the registration notches are correctly matched together.
2. Pour clay slip through one hole in the back of the mould. Do not allow the slip to fall directly on to the inner surface of the mould, but pour so that it runs down the side of the filling hole. If the slip hits the design's surface directly on pouring, there is danger that the clay particles will separate out, forming a hard, dense, glaze resistant surface directly opposite to the filling hole, which may only be seen after the tile is fired and glazing takes place.
3. When the mould, including the filling hole, is full, it should be left for approximately 20 minutes. The time for casting will vary with the thickness desired for the tile and with the consistency of the slip. As the mould absorbs the water from the casting slip the level of slip in the filling hole will slowly fall: this should be topped up from time to time.

   In the case of casting a solid tile a reservoir of slip over the filling holes may be necessary. This may be gained by building a clay wall around both holes. There is no need to pour out excess slip when making solid tiles; the cast is left until the filling hole is solid, then the tile may be removed.

   With hollow casting, the slip must be removed from the mould after the desired thickness for the tile is achieved. Empty the slip from one hole and allow air to enter the cast through the other hole.
4. After emptying excess slip or, in the case of solid tiles, after the filling hole has become solid with slip, the cast should be left a short time to complete the drying process. The cast tile may be removed from the mould when all tackiness has disappeared from the inner surface of the solid clay slip. The excess clay in the filling hole should be cut away before removing the tile from the mould.
5. The back of the mould will invariably be easily removed, but difficulty may be experienced when removing the cast tile from the front of the mould.

Gentle taps on the sides of the mould, applied with the palm of the hand, should free any parts of the tile that stick to the mould's inner surface. If the tile does not release itself after tapping, leave it a whole day to dry before further attempts are made.

6. After the tile has been removed from the mould it should be left until bone dry before any further work is done on it. Hollow tiles may be dried easily by laying them out on flat boards, with no special precautions necessary as they are unlikely to warp. Solid cast tiles should be dried with the same precautions taken as for handmade tiles, being either stood on edge or laid out on racking.
7. Finishing or fettling should only be carried out on bone dry tiles. It will be found easy to gently scrape them and sponge away any excess clay from the seams formed by the mould.

MIXING CASTING SLIP

Ingredients

1. Clay, either plastic or powdered.
2. Soda ash and sodium silicate. These are known as de-flocculants.
3. Water.

Clay

Any clay may be used to make a casting slip. The proportions in which ingredients are mixed are determined by the type of clay used and so is the method of mixing. Powdered clay is simpler to mix with water than wet plastic clay; this should not, however, be the sole consideration in the choice of clay to be used. Other considerations should take precedent, e.g. availability of clay and familiarity with its firing qualities; the type of ware to be made, stoneware or earthenware, etc.

Soda ash and sodium silicate

The action of these 'de-flocculants' in the casting slip is such as to allow a fluid liquid to be made by breaking down small lumps or clinging particles of clay.

De-flocculants allow the slip to become fluid with less water than would be necessary without their use. After all ingredients have been thoroughly mixed either by hand or blunger, the slip should be passed through a 100-size sieve and left for two or three days before use. This space of time will help ensure that the de-flocculants have done their work.

After casting has taken place, there will remain scraps of dry casting slip. These may be used again with a new recipe that compensates for the de-flocculant that is present in the scraps. Once a clay has been made into a casting slip it will have lost its value as a plastic clay, e.g. for throwing or modelling.

Soda ash or sodium carbonate

Promotes good drainage of casting slip from mould. If too much soda ash is used, the cast shape may be flabby and will not dry properly after draining.

Soda ash should be used when plastic clay is made into a casting slip.

Sodium silicate or water glass

Promotes fluidity and creates a harder cast than soda ash.

Sodium silicate may be purchased in various concentrations; these are measured in Degrees Twaddell (°T.); 140°T., 100°T., 75°T., are the usual three grades that are used for making casting slip. Each has its own value for particular clays.

It is usual to find both soda ash and sodium silicate in most casting slips.

The best way of getting the correct recipe for any one type of clay is to ask the supplier of the clay for their recommendations.

Water

When mixing casting slip it will be found advantageous to use warm water to dissolve the de-flocculants and to help in breaking the clay down, into a smooth liquid.

Casting slip recipes vary with the clay used. The suppliers of the clay will normally give a recommended recipe, but if this is not obtainable, the following examples will help in experiments to prove a good recipe:

3 Nineteenth-century tile with copper plate engraved design, transferred to the tile's surface, with underglaze painted colours

1. Wet, white earthenware clay 100 lb.
   140°T. sodium silicate 8 oz.
   Water 10 pints
2. Wet, plastic stoneware clay 100 lb.
   140°T. sodium silicate 3 oz.
   Soda ash 2 oz.
   Water 12 pints

PRESSMOULD TILES

The procedure for making a pressmould is exactly the same as that for making a slipcast mould, with the following exceptions.

1. Make the mould stronger by increasing its all-round thickness by at least 1 in.
2. No back piece is necessary to the mould.
3. When making the pressmould it will be found useful, but not absolutely necessary, to place two strips of thin plastic, wood or glass along two opposite edges of the mould. These strips should be approximately ½ in. wide and almost as long as the edge of the mould along which they run. They should be placed in the gap between the model and the wooden box and helped to retain this position by applying a thin coating of clay slip to one of their sides. This side of the strip should be placed in contact with the smooth casting surface.

   When the mould is used, these strips prevent wear and tear on its surface that may be caused when scraping off excess clay, in the pressmould technique, as follows:

FILLING THE PRESSMOULD

1. Wedge a lump of clay to extrude all air pockets. The amount of clay used should be sufficient to fill the mould plus some in excess.
2. Make the clay into a round ball, smoothing out any cracks or blemishes that may be on its surface.
3. Place ball of clay in the mould and press down on the centre of the ball with the palm of the hand. Repeat downward pressure with the thumbs, working outwards from the centre of the ball of clay. If this is done carefully, all air spaces between clay and mould should be expelled. When the clay is nearly touching the edge of the design, start to press down with the thumbs,

working the clay into one corner. The pressure should now be applied along the sides of the tile, working from corner to corner.

4. On being satisfied that the mould is fully charged with clay, all excess clay is trimmed off with a wire or narrow-bladed knife.

   The hollows in the back of the tile, left by pressing the clay, may now be filled, taking care that air is not trapped between layers. Scrape off all clay standing proud of the mould's edges. This is done by pulling a 'straight edge' made of wood across the surface of the mould and the pressed clay tile, starting from the centre and working outwards in varying directions. This scraping action may cause damage to the mould unless protective strips are set along the edges when the mould is being made.

   Tiles of up to 1 in. thick may be made solid. Tiles of any greater thickness should have some clay taken from their backs to form a neatly modelled hollow. Hollow-back tiles will dry more evenly and are less prone to cracking when fired.

5. The completed tile may be removed from the mould after some time has been given for the clay to stiffen by drying. However, it may be found that simple designs can be removed immediately after pressing, especially if the plaster mould is completely dry. Drying pressed tiles ready for firing is the same procedure used for handmade tiles.

SANDCAST TILES

This is a similar technique to slipcasting from plaster moulds: a mould is made from sand which absorbs the moisture from the slip. It must be stated that sand moulds are not as efficient as plaster moulds and the control and precision gained from plaster cannot be expected with sand. Other particular differences are:

(a) Longer casting times are necessary.
(b) Designs to be repeated will all differ in some way.
(c) The sand imposes the same surface quality on all designs.

MAKING THE SANDCAST MOULD

1. Make a wooden box with an open top, 4–6 in. deep, length of sides to exceed the dimensions of the tile by at least 2 in.

2. Take enough silver sand to fill box three-quarters full. Add enough water to this sand to make the particles cling together. Do not add too much water as this will prevent the maximum absorption of moisture from the clay slip when casting takes place.
3. Place sand in box and tamp down to an even firm surface.
4. An impression may now be made in the sand, forming the design of the tile. Any object may be used to create the impression and with practice a crisp image may be made.
5. Slowly fill impressed design with clay slip, filling only up to the edge limits of the tile. If any slip spills over the edge limits, leave until tile is dry, then trim. The slip used for sand casting should be much thicker than that used in plaster moulds; with some slips it may be found helpful to add grog as a stiffening agent. When the mould is full of slip it should be left to dry in a warm room or drying cupboard and may take a full day or more to stiffen sufficiently for the clay tile to be easily removed from the sand mould.
6. After drying remove tile from sand and lay out on flat board or drying racks. It will be found that some of the sand will be sticking to the surface of the tile; this sand should not be removed from the tile until the clay is bone dry. The removal of sand is achieved by sweeping the tile's surface with a stiff brush.
7. There is a tendency for sandcast tiles to warp upwards at each corner whilst drying in the mould. This fault may be counteracted by laying a flat slab of plaster over the tile whilst it is still in the mould. Sandcast tiles made to fit together in a panel invariably need cutting to size when bone dry. Designs made in this fashion should be such as to allow for this final edge trimming, which may be carried out by using a 'Surform' blade.

EXTRUDED TILES

As the name implies, tiles may be made by squeezing or 'extruding' clay through a shaped hole, cut out of a metal or plastic plate. The hole is cut to the cross section of the finished tile.

In order to extrude tiles it is necessary to have a wad box or pugmill.

The width of tile is dependent on the size of wad box or pugmill, but the length may be any measurement which is easy to handle.

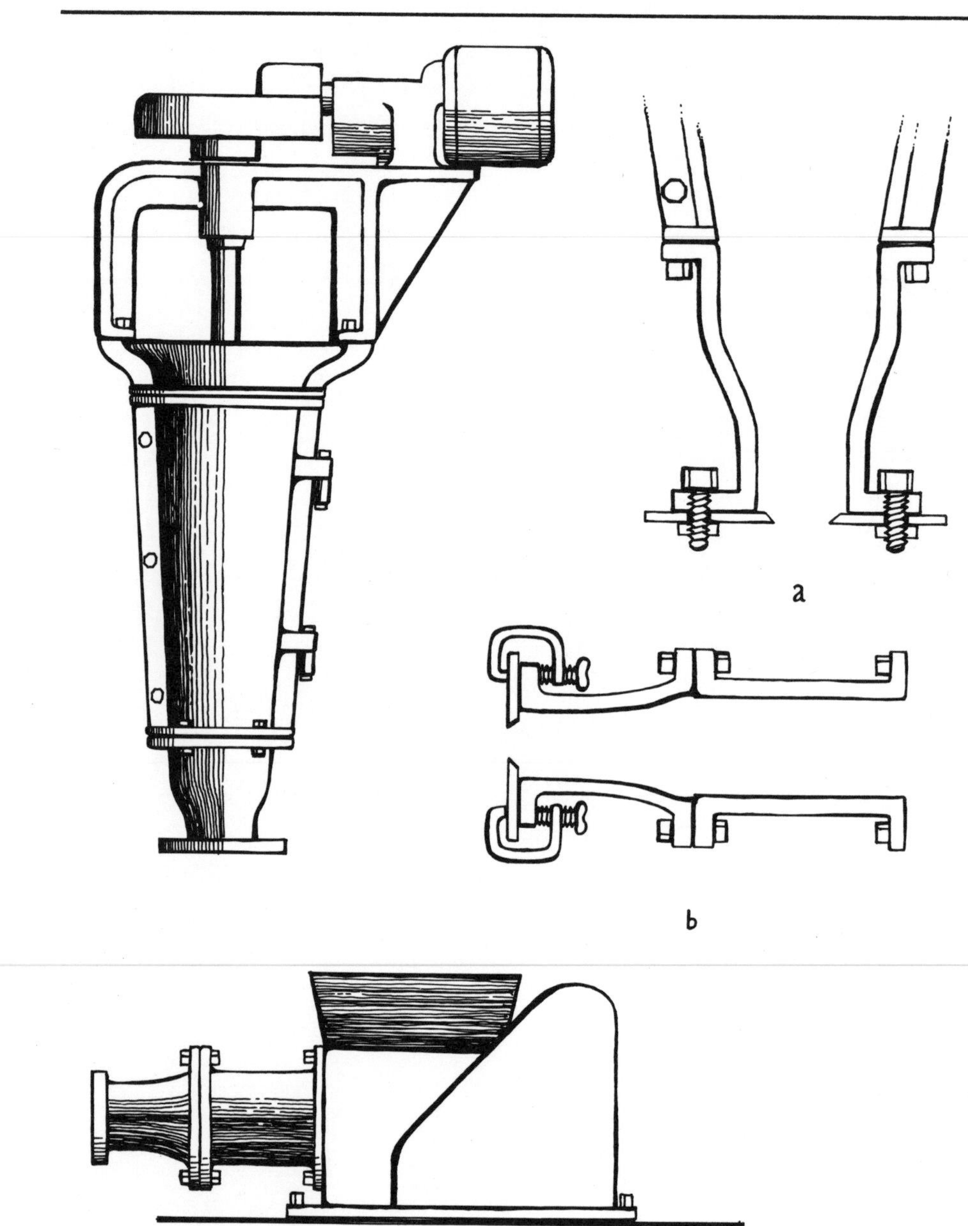

Fig. 22. Fixing a die plate to a pugmill

MAKING THE DIEPLATE OR TEMPLATE

The plate may be made from any sheet metal or sheet acrylic plastic.

If metal is used, it should be steel and $\frac{1}{8}$ in. to $\frac{1}{4}$ in. in thickness. If plastic is used, it should be at least $\frac{1}{4}$ in. or more in thickness.

The majority of wad boxes require a circular dieplate. These may sometimes be purchased as blanks from the manufacturers of the wad box.

When a pugmill is used for extruding it is necessary to devise a method of holding the dieplate in position at the extrusion nozzle of the machine. Some pugmills have threaded holes tapped in the nozzle and it is a simple matter to drill corresponding holes (Fig. 22) in the dieplate which may be used to bolt the plate in position. If threaded holes are not present the plate will have to be clamped to the pugmill (Fig. 22). As pugmills differ in design, there is no set procedure for clamping. This problem has to be solved in accordance with the demands of each situation.

The hole that will form the design is first roughly drilled out of the plate then sawn to a more accurate profile. It should then be filed to a finish, putting a bevel all round the edge of the design (Fig. 23a).

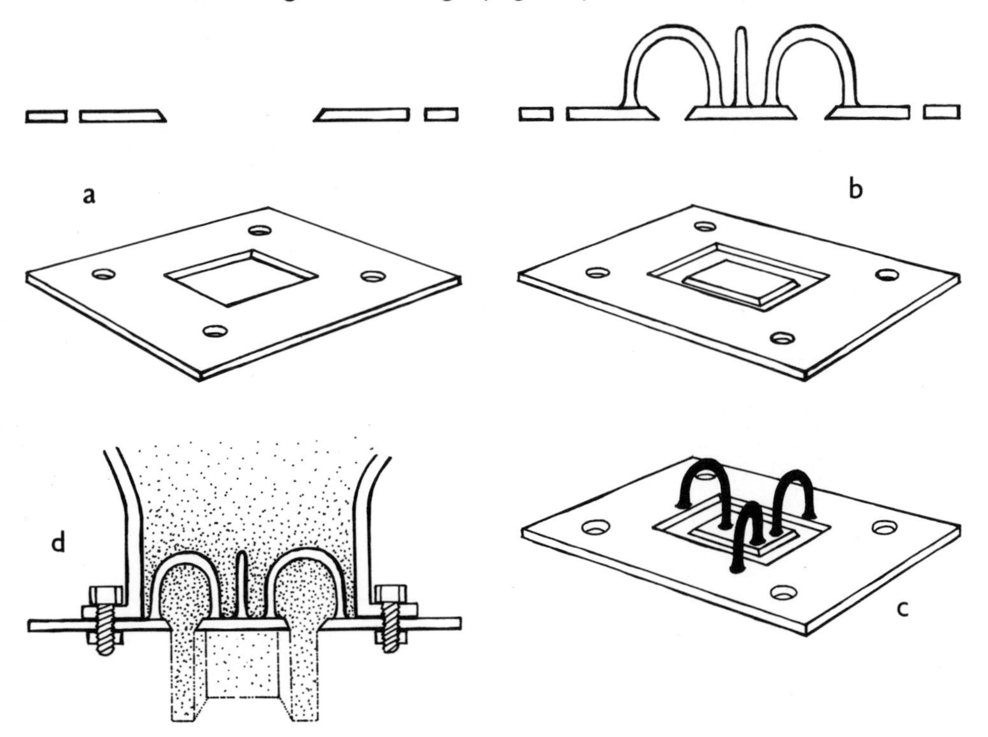

Fig. 23. Making dieplates for extrusion

It is obvious that plastic is the easiest material to work when making dieplates but some designs may require metal dieplates in order to withstand the heavy pressures placed on them whilst being used. Extra holes may have to be pierced in the dieplate to relieve some of the back pressure set up by pugmills when extruding. These should be placed in such a position as to exclude interference with the designed extruded shape.

EXTRUDING WITH A WAD BOX

Place the dieplate in position at the extrusion nozzle of the wad box. Fill forcing cylinder with clay, ensuring that as little air as possible is trapped in the clay. Apply pressure with the piston in a slow and continuous fashion. The length of clay extruded in this way should exceed that of the finished tile, which allows for trimming after the clay extrusion has become leather-hard.

EXTRUDING WITH A PUGMILL

The dieplate is clamped or bolted to the extrusion nozzle of the machine. If the machine is driven by an electric motor it will be necessary to switch it on and off between extruded lengths. With vertical pugmills care must be taken when handling the lengths of clay if warpage is to be avoided; after extrusion, lay out complete lengths of clay on flat boards until leather-hard, then trim to size required for tile. With horizontal pugmills a flat board should be supported in a horizontal position, extending from the extrusion nozzle. This board should have oil applied to its surface to enable the extruded clay to slide easily over its surface. When extrusion takes place from either vertical or horizontal mills the clay length may have a tendency to curl; this is overcome by guiding the clay with the hand, holding the first 2 or 3 in. of the extrusion.

CUTTING EXTRUSION TILES TO SHAPE

When the clay extrusions are leather-hard they may be cut to the desired length of tile. If the tiles are to vary in length they may be measured and cut with a wire harp or narrow-bladed knife. To cut regular repeated shapes it will be necessary to use a wooden jig (Fig. 24).

Experimentation will show that many complex designs may be produced by cutting across the extruded length at different angles (Fig. 25).

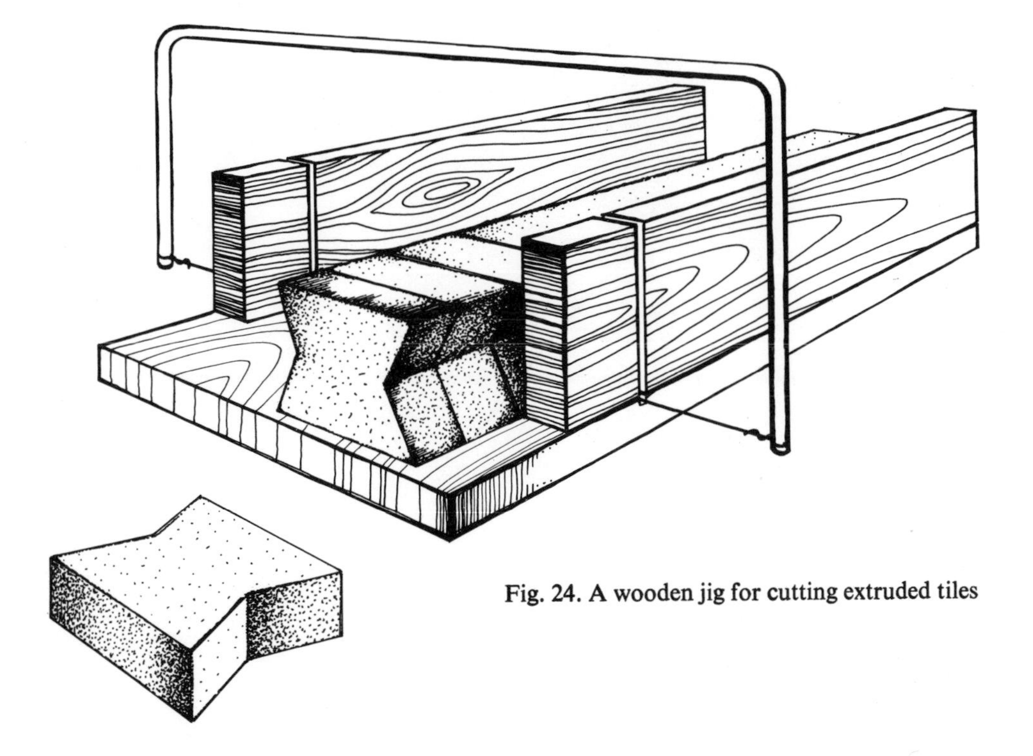

Fig. 24. A wooden jig for cutting extruded tiles

HOLLOW EXTRUSIONS

Hollow tiles may be made using a special dieplate. This plate must always be made of metal, preferably steel.

1. The designed hole is cut from the metal plate as for solid extrusions.
2. A piece of the same metal is now cut, conforming to the shape of the hollow cavity needed in the tile (Fig. 23b).
3. Two or three pieces of 'U'-shaped metal rod are used to connect the two cut metal plates. These are welded in position (Fig. 23c).
4. The plate is fitted to the pugmill with bolts or by clamping. The connecting 'U'-shaped rods should be placed inside the extrusion nozzle (Fig. 23d).
5. Stiffer than normal clay should be used if possible when extruding hollow forms.
6. Care must be taken when cutting extruded lengths to shape if distortion is to be avoided—very thin strong wire is recommended.

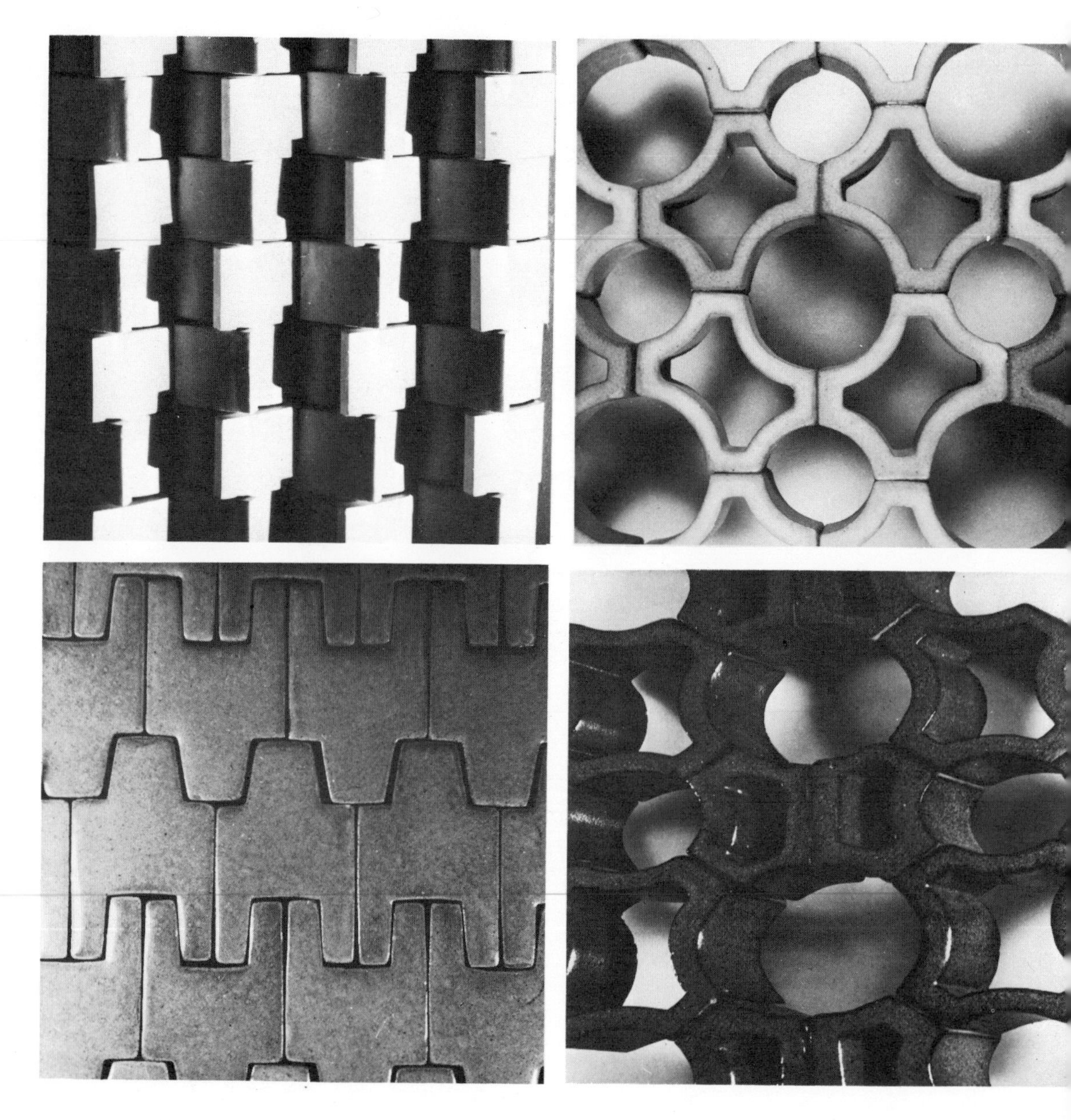

Fig. 25. Examples of extruded tiles

4 · The Use and Decoration of Factory-made Tiles

If one's interest is solely that of decorating tiles or the means to make the tiles are not at hand, then the factory-made tile will solve many problems.

The pottery industry manufactures an enormous range of tile products. The types available vary in size from the 4¼ × 4¼ in. sq. domestic tile to the large 2 ft. × 1 ft. exterior architectural cladding tile. Shapes vary as much as size, from the square and rectangular to the complex 'ogee' interlocking tile (Fig. 26).

At first sight the colour range of commercial tiles seems limited, but if enquiries are made direct to the manufacturers, the colour range will be found to extend beyond that of the dull green and creams stocked by many retail outlets.

Glazed ceramic tiles

Designs may be built up from the single coloured tile. These can be arranged in various compositions. The finished effect will of course be dependent on the variety of tiles used, their shape, size and colour. An extension of their use is found by cutting them into shape or by re-colouring them.

The commercial tile's smooth, regular surface presents an excellent opportunity to use most graphic techniques and imagery. These may range from the hand-drawn to the mechanically produced; lithographed and silkscreened.

The ease with which decoration may be applied to the tile's surface can create confidence. The fact that the tile may be wiped clean and the work started afresh, without too much loss of time or materials, helps to strengthen this confidence and increases the scope for experimentation.

Firing may be carried out without the fear of warpage, although I have found that one type of 'Do-it-yourself' tile tends to warp when fired.

The temperature range for firing most commercially-made glazed tiles extends up to 1,150°C. This allows the following list of techniques to be employed:

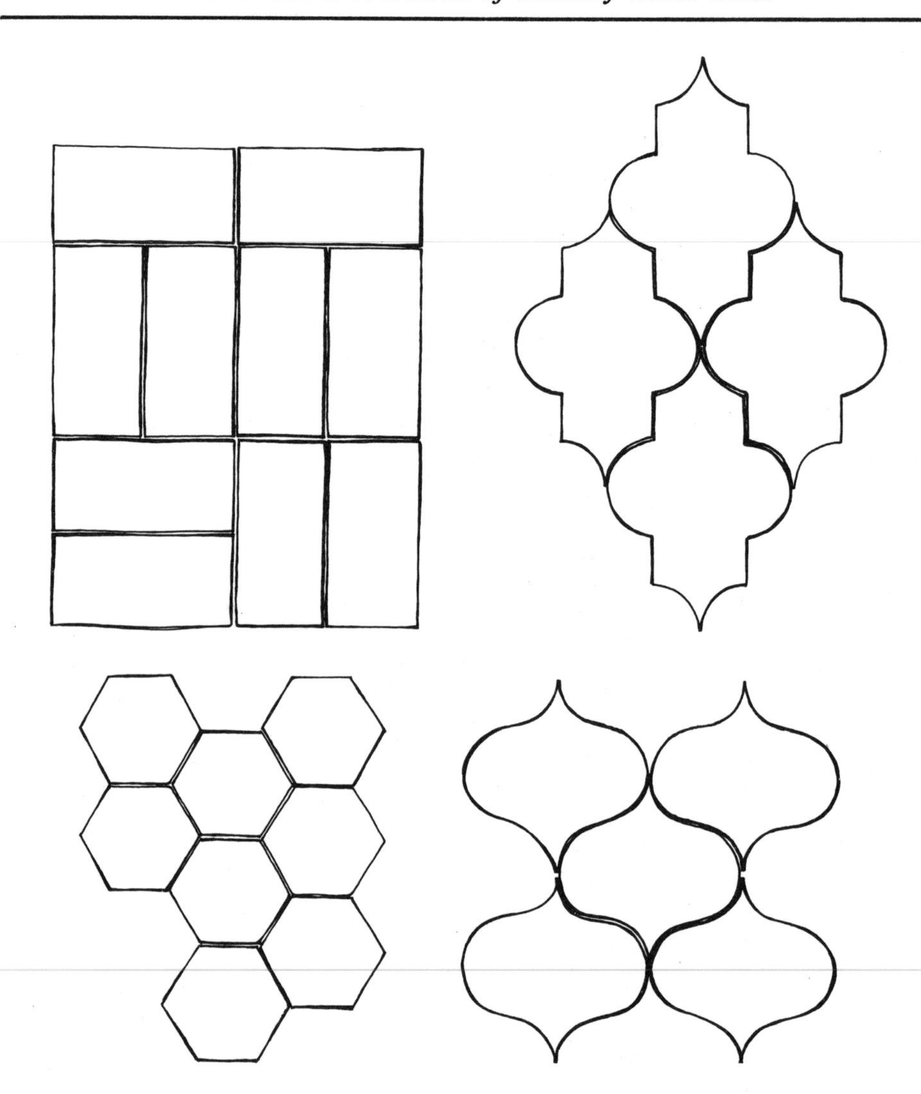

Fig. 26. Shapes of factory-made tiles

1. Enamels, 700°C. to 800°C.
2. Majolica glazes, 900°C. to 1,060°C.
3. Earthenware glazes, 1,000°C. to 1,150°C.
4. On-glaze colours (majolica or faience), 900°C. to 1,150°C.
5. Underglaze colours (re-glazed), 900°C. to 1,150°C.

When using any of the above techniques, care in firing must be observed, following these directions:

1. Initial heat rise in kiln should be slow and steady.
2. Good ventilation of kiln at all times to prevent accidental reducing conditions.
3. No strong draughts of cold air should be allowed into the kiln.
4. Cooling should be slow and steady.
5. Kiln should not be opened too soon after cooling, preferably not above 150°C. to 200°C.

If conditions 1, 3, 4 and 5 are not controlled, there is the danger that some of the tiles in the firing may crack. If condition 2 is not controlled, the colour quality of the design may be impaired or radically changed.

Re-glazing commercial tiles

Unexpected results may be achieved when ready-glazed tiles have a second or even third layer of glaze applied to their surface.

Some of the effects gained in this way will be detrimental to the design, but sometimes the finished glazed effect can be controlled and in this way it will enlarge the palette of glaze quality and the means of expression.

As a general rule the re-glazing will always change the colour and quality of both the existing glaze and the one applied to its surface. When re-glazing the following should be observed:

1. Remove all dust and grease marks from the tile's surface. These may cause resistance to the applied glaze and upset the smoothness of application.
2. If the glaze is applied with a spray gun, lay tile on a horizontal surface and allow the glaze to fall over its surface. Do not aim the spray gun directly at its surface, or hold the gun too near the surface. This will exclude the possibility of the power of the spray blowing the glaze over the tile in waves.

3. When pouring glaze over the tile surface, try as far as is possible to completely cover the tile's area in one movement. Hold the tile at a steep angle and pour the glaze along its top edge, allowing the glaze to run to the bottom edge and across all the tile's surface in one continuous movement. If any glaze runs over the back of the tile it should be cleaned off after the glaze on the top surface has dried.
4. In most cases it is advisable to add a small amount of liquid gum arabic to the glaze before applying it to the tile. When the glaze has dried the gum will give some protection against its being accidentally scratched or flaking away from the tile's surface.
5. Always test glazes used for this technique. They should always be tested over the surface on which they will eventually be applied.

The requirements for other techniques are described in other relevant chapters.

Unglazed commercial tiles

It is possible to purchase, from some manufacturers, unglazed biscuit tiles. These tiles may be decorated in a similar fashion to tiles that are handmade. The range of tiles to be dealt with here does not include those left unglazed to order, but deals with those unglazed tiles that were designed for purposes not needing a glaze, e.g. quarry tiles (floor tiles), or roof tiles.

Most unglazed tiles are thicker and cruder in finish than glazed cladding tiles. The reason for this difference is that they are usually designed for heavier and less exact uses than that of finishing wall surfaces. They are therefore best used when forceful and direct design qualities are required, or when their eventual use demands weight and strength.

The colour range of unglazed tiles is invariably limited to subdued tones of blacks, browns, terracotta red and buff colours. Their colour range should not impede their use if opaque glazes are used to cover the body colour.

Firing unglazed tiles demands the same precautions as those for glazed tiles—a slow rise and fall in temperature. As a further precaution, they should be thoroughly dried before use; this is necessary, due to the fact that the tiles may well have been stored open to the weather, by builders' merchants, and any absorbed moisture must be dried out to prevent possible cracking when the tile is refired.

Special shapes

Commercial tiles need a selection of specially designed shapes to enlarge and complete their usefulness. Some of these 'specials' may be seen in Fig. 27 and will possibly be found useful to complete murals etc., or may be used by themselves in creating free-form compositions.

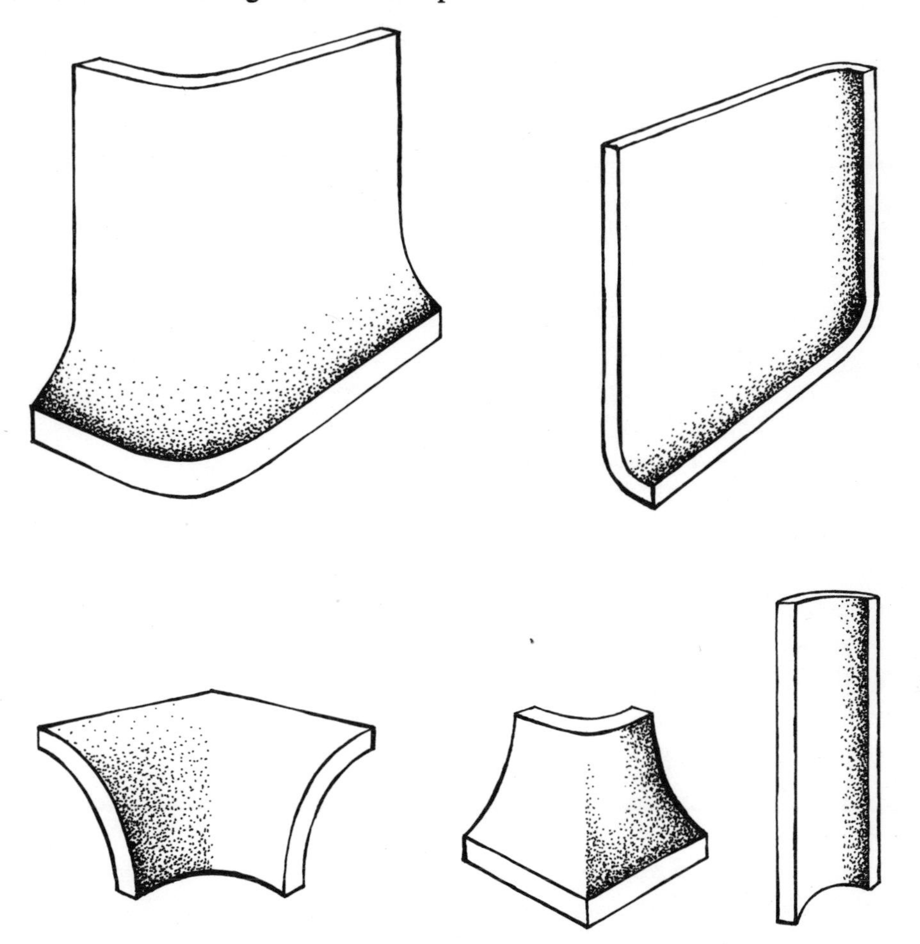

Fig. 27. Special shapes in factory-made tiles

Cutting commercial tiles

It may be found necessary to cut tiles down to a smaller size in order that they will fit a limited space, or so that their shape fulfils a design requirement.

The most easily cut tiles are those having a thickness of $\frac{1}{4}$ in. or less and cutting may be done in the following manner:

STRAIGHT CUTS

1. Draw a line, with a pencil or sharp wax crayon, along the position of the cut.
2. Lay a steel rule or hardwood straight edge along the line to act as a guide for the cutting tool.
3. Use a tungsten carbide tipped cutting tool and following the drawn line, scratch a deep groove in the tile's surface. Tungsten tools may be purchased from any hardware store. If one is not to hand, a wheel-type glass cutting tool may be used. More pressure than normal will be necessary when scratching grooves with this type of cutter.
4. After scratching line of cut, lay tile on flat surface and place two matchsticks, one under each end of the scratched groove. Apply even pressure downward on each side of the groove. The tile should snap along the line of the scratched groove. If it does not break immediately the groove should be deepened and pressure reapplied.
5. Any raggedness at the cut edge may be smoothed down with a block of medium carborundum.
6. If thick tiles are to be cut it will be found necessary to gradually chip away part of the tile, working slowly up to the line of the groove.

CUTTING IRREGULAR SHAPES

The shape to be cut is scratched in outline, with a tungsten-tipped tool, in the surface of the tile; a metal or wooden template should be used as a guide. The excess tile is now carefully snipped away with a pair of pliers or pincers, working slowly to the scratched groove.

Holes may be cut in tiles by first drilling a pilot hole with a masonry bit and then snipping the tile away outwards towards the desired shape.

Mosaic tessera may be cut from tiles by scratching a grid pattern of squares across the tile's surface and then snapping off first strips and then the mosaic squares. Before any actual cutting work is commenced it is advisable to practise on a spare tile.

General notes on commercial tiles

Although most manufacturers produce visually similar tiles, there is often a great difference in their technical make-up. The following points should therefore be noted.

1. No two different makes of white or similarly coloured tiles necessarily have the same glaze. They may also differ slightly in size and thickness.
2. The capacity to withstand refiring tends to decline with each firing and with the increase in the thickness of the glaze.
3. Stemming from the above points, always use the same make of tile, especially in one design project. This will ensure that effects gained by re-glazing and decorating will be consistent.
4. Do not take for granted that because a tile's original glaze has not crazed it will not do so when further glazes are applied. Testing glazes before the work commences will prepare one for such technical defects.

5 · Decorating Tiles with Glazes

The use of glazes for decorating a tile's surface can create qualities ranging from the precise and linear to the flowing and expansive. If used intelligently, glazes may cater for design attitudes as far apart as the 'hopefully accidental' and the 'precisely formulated'.

Methods of application

PAINTING GLAZES

The major problem when using glazes for decoration is controlling the correct thickness of application.

Painted glazes give ample opportunity to experience the results gained by varying thickness of one glaze.

The true nature of a glaze is not seen until it has been fired, only experience of glazes before and after firing will give full control of the correct thickness of application. As a general rule, the colour of a painted glaze is inconsistent; it varies with the type of brush used for painting and the viscosity or thickness of the raw liquid glaze. To put it very simply, brush strokes always show when the glaze has been fired. This fact has to be faced when designing a painted glaze decoration. The brush stroke marks cannot be ignored and must be incorporated into the design. Hard bristle-brushes will usually emphasize the stroke mark; soft hair brushes will minimize, but not overcome, the stroke mark. Experiment will show effects left by different brushes. Different combinations of brushes, speed of stroke and thickness of glaze can give an infinite variety of qualities.

The usual interpretation of 'painted' work is often associated with picture making in artists' oil colour; this type of picture making is only one of the many design ideas that may be executed with painted glazes. In order to increase one's vocabulary of painted effects, some of the following suggestions for experiment may be used;

4 Raised linear design infilled with coloured glazes. Nineteenth-century tile

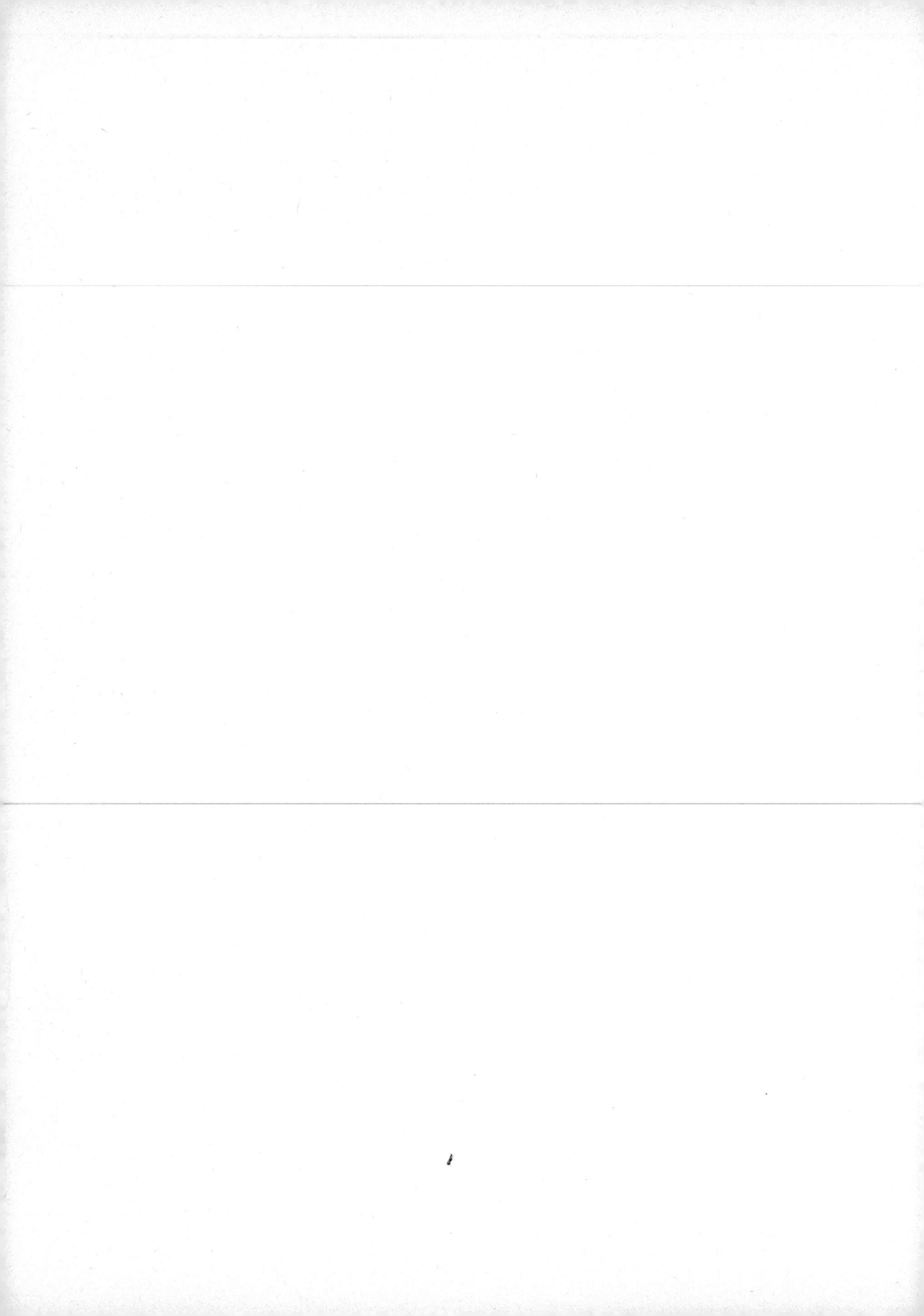

1. Use any type of brush and paint thick glaze in single horizontal strokes across the tile's surface. Vary the speed of stroke, the direction of its movement and the thickness of glaze. Start with slow, deliberate movements; develop these into fast spontaneous strokes.
2. Cover the tile's surface with short strokes of glaze that run into each other at different angles. Repeat this process using different types of brush.
3. Paint a lattice design across the tile's surface, noting how the change of direction of the overpainting affects the shapes made by the brush.
4. Hold brush at varying angles to the tile's surface and press downward, relieve the pressure with no lateral movement. This may be repeated to create a spot pattern or an all over covering of glaze on the tile's surface.
5. Use combinations of the above and any other strokes. Always fire the experiments as it is only after firing that the work done by the brush will be seen clearly. After firing, it will be found that the thickness of glaze has varied and the intensity of the colour changes with the thickness of the glaze. It is this quality that will have to be noted and used when painting glazes.

SPRAYING GLAZES

To spray glazes it is not necessary to possess sophisticated compressors and spray guns. Many useful effects may be gained with the use of a mouth spray or insecticide spray gun.

It is very important to guard against inhaling the excess spray of glaze. The work should be carried out in the open air or in a specially constructed spray booth, fitted with an extractor fan. A protective mask should be worn over mouth and nose.

Preparation of materials for spraying should be thorough, the glaze used must be sieved through a 120-mesh screen to clear all lumps from the liquid. Failure to sieve glazes and to keep the spray gun clean can lead to frustrating delays when the nozzle of the gun becomes blocked; a dirty spray gun can also cause contamination of one glaze by another.

The surface of the tiles being sprayed must be wiped clean of dirt, dust and grease marks. When spraying glazed tiles, remember that their surface is non-porous and guard against blowing the sprayed wet glaze off the tile by holding the gun too near its surface. Glazed tiles should be laid flat whilst being sprayed, allowing the glaze to fall evenly over the surface. Biscuit tiles that are porous may be held in the hand when being sprayed. In both cases it will be necessary to move the tile in a circular motion to help in the even distribution of the glaze.

It will be found useful to lay glazed tiles on a plaster block when spraying. This block will dry out the excess glaze and prevent it from running under the tile. As an alternative to a plaster block, the tile may be propped above the spraying surface with pieces of kiln furniture.

Spraying a glaze may be used as a technique for decorating in its own right, or it may be used in conjunction with other techniques where control over glazed areas is necessary, stencilled glazes etc.

STENCILLED GLAZES

The technique for applying glazes with the aid of a stencil is similar to that employed in stencilling paints on paper: with the following provisions:

1. The stencil should be cut from a material able to withstand saturation by the water in the glaze. (Waterproof paper or thin cardboard.) If absorbent material is used it should be dampened before laying it on the tile, in order to prevent any cockling or expansion of its shape, which will distort the design.
2. If it is intended to stencil one glaze over another, gum arabic should be added to the underglaze in the proportion of 1 tablespoon of gum to approximately 1 pint of glaze. When the glaze containing the gum arabic dries, a hard scratchproof surface is formed, over which may be laid stencils and subsequent layers of glaze. Dampened stencils should not be used for this work as they tend to soften the first layer of glaze.
3. If possible, stencils should be retained in position on the tile's surface with either sticky tape or thin rolls of stiff clay. This is especially true if the glaze is to be sprayed over the stencil, with the possibility of blowing the stencil out of its true position.

   The stencil should not be removed until the glaze has dried. This excludes the possibility of the wet glaze running under the stencil and distorting edges of the design.
4. Any method may be employed for applying the glaze over the stencil. Spraying is by far the most efficient, as it gives an even layer of glaze. Pro-

viding the spray gun is held away from the design and the glaze is allowed to fall downward, no movement of the stencil should occur.

Stippling and painting with a sponge or brush have the disadvantage that physical contact with the stencil could cause movement and smudge the design. The marks left by sponge or brush when stippling will show after firing and this must be allowed for in the design.

5. Stencilled designs may be executed over a single tile or over a panel composed of a number of tiles. If the latter is used, care must be taken that glaze does not run under the stencil at the joints of the tiles. Any glaze that does move under the stencil should be scraped away after the stencil has been removed and the glaze is dry.
6. Designs composed purely of stencilled shapes tend to look unfinished and empty of interest. One reason for this is that very little detail may be drawn with stencils. It will be found that other techniques may be used to create details after making the larger, bolder shapes by stencilling.

POOLED GLASS AND GLAZES

Glazes are normally applied in thin layers, but they may also be used in thick pools as long as they are contained in cavities or retained by modelled walls on the tile's surface.

Pooled glazes may only be used on handmade tiles that are designed to receive them. The main advantages gained by using glazes thickly, is an added depth of colour and a jewel-like quality that many transparent glazes possess when applied in pools.

The main disadvantages are as follows:

1. Pooled glazes invariably craze after firing.
2. Devitrification sometimes occurs on cooling, resulting in a dull or crusty glaze surface.
3. The extra thickness of glaze combined with crazing will often crack the body of the tile.
4. A retaining wall or cavity is always necessary and tends to reduce design possibilities.
5. Only transparent glazes are useful. Opaque glazes do not give the thick glass qualities desired of this technique.

An alternative to using thick glaze is to use powdered glass. Almost any glass can be useful, e.g. bottles, window glass and glass mosaic pieces. If glass is used, the following points should be noted:

1. Different types of glass may have different melting temperatures.
2. Some glass loses its colour after firing.
3. Devitrification may occur on cooling, and tends to happen more frequently than with glazes.
4. Glass may be cut to shape and placed in position on the tile's surface. Alternatively it may be ground into small pieces or to a powder. This is particularly useful when small details are required.
5. Unlike glazes, glass is usually added to a tile in a dry powdered form. When fired, it fuses together, forming approximately half its original powdered volume. It will be seen from this that enough glass must be present to create the volume required.

DOUBLE GLAZING

Glazes may be used side by side on a tile's surface or applied one over another. Placing one glaze on another will usually create a third colour and texture, e.g. a transparent blue glaze under a transparent yellow will produce a green colour. Changes in glaze qualities or textures may be achieved by using an opaque glaze with a transparent glaze. The variations that may be had with a small number of glazes are endless and tests must always be carried out to judge the usefulness of any combination of glazes. The following precautions should be noted when double glazing:

1. Each glaze has its proper thickness for application, but when two glazes are applied, one over another, the resulting thickness of glaze will be approximately double that which is normal for either glaze. It can be seen from this that the two glazes will have to be thinned, so reducing the thickness of the double glazed area. Do not thin out the glaze too much, otherwise any single glazed areas will be too thin and the quality of the glazes will be lost.
2. Allow the first glaze applied to dry before applying the second. Do not allow the first glaze to become bone dry, as this will cause the second application of glaze to blister and possibly flake off. The cause of this fault is that the moisture from the second glaze forces the air out of the first bone dry glaze and in doing so disrupts the evenness of the second layer of glaze.

3. Care must be taken that the two or more glazes used in the operation do not become accidentally mixed. When pouring one glaze over another, use a clean bowl to catch the excess glaze, which may then be inspected for any signs of contamination. If it appears that only a very little glaze has become intermixed, this may generally be overlooked, as most glazes can absorb some intermixing without losing their original colour or quality. Some glazes will stain others very easily: cobalt and copper glazes in particular, and special care should be taken when these are used.

Types of glaze and their use

For convenience, glazes may be divided into two main categories, earthenware and stoneware, and these may then be subdivided in the following manner:

EARTHENWARE GLAZES

1. Low temperature (approximately 800°C. to 1,000°C.).
2. High temperature (approximately 1,000°C. to 1,150°C.).

STONEWARE GLAZES

1. Reduced stoneware (approximately 1,250°C. to 1,300°C.).
2. Oxidized stoneware (approximately 1,150°C. to 1,300°C.).

Further glaze divisions may be had by examining their qualities, generally as follows:

1. Transparent. Clear and Coloured.
2. Opaque. White and Coloured.
3. Glossy in 1. and 2.
4. Matt in 2.
5. Lead glazes.
6. Alkaline glazes.
7. Crystalline glazes.
8. Ash glazes.

The range of variation found in glazes is enormous and the subject demands a complete study by itself. This knowledge may be gained from specialist publications and practical experience. What is considered herein as important, are the general points of departure for the successful use of glazes on tiles, and the main uses to which any glaze mentioned may be applied. No one potter can ever be expected to attain the complete range of glaze effects. It can only be expected that the individual may come to terms with the materials at his immediate disposal and that general statements may be weighed in the light of individual experience.

LOW-TEMPERATURE EARTHENWARE GLAZES 800°C. TO 1,000°C.

Main points of interest

1. Compared with the colours normally associated with earthenware glazes, low-temperature glazes can give extremely bright hues, together with those colours considered normal.
2. Many of the really bright coloured glazes have to be purchased ready mixed from glaze manufacturers. This is due to the finely balanced chemical makeup of the glaze, which is easily upset by slight inaccuracies in mixing.
3. Low-temperature glazes tend to be soft in firing and are therefore liable to run down vertical surfaces. They are excellent for the flat surface of tilework.
4. If low-temperature glazes are applied too thinly there is usually a loss of quality and colour. This is especially true of bright red glazes that have been purchased ready mixed.
5. Low-temperature glazes give excellent results, when used as pooled glazes.

HIGH-TEMPERATURE EARTHENWARE GLAZES 1,000°C. TO 1,150°C.

Main points of interest

1. Extensive range of colour and qualities, that may be supplemented by using low-fired glazes, enamels, on-glaze and underglaze colours.
2. May be intermixed, but only after experimentation.
3. Are stable on vertical surfaces unless extremely overfired.
4. A useful colour range may be made by simply adding metallic oxides to a basic transparent glaze or an opaque glaze. Glaze stains purchased from manufacturers will enlarge this basic palette.
5. High-temperature glazes may be mixed from recipes in most studio con-

ditions and, unlike ready-mixed low-temperature glaze, the raw materials are reasonably cheap, and simple to use.

6. They may be applied to the tile's surface by many techniques.

REDUCED-STONEWARE GLAZES 1,250°C. TO 1,300°C.

Main points of interest

1. Gives a good range of muted colours with the exception of some glazes that contain copper, which give pinks to reds.
2. Often richly textured with broken colour that enhances certain types of modelled form on a tile's surface.
3. Imparts a natural relationship between the clay tile and its glazed surface, which is often difficult to achieve with earthenware glazes.
4. Basic ingredients of most stoneware glaze recipes are cheap and simple to use in studio conditions.
5. Normally should not be used on commercially made tiles and should only be applied to clays that are capable of withstanding high temperatures and reducing atmosphere. Some unglazed commercial tiles may be able to withstand these firing conditions. But it will be necessary to fire a trial piece.
6. Glaze is normally applied thickly and it often remains thick after firing. This may obscure small modelled details.
7. Stoneware clays and glazes are impervious to moisture and work intended for external weathering conditions may be carried out in this technique.
8. Muted colours tend to limit terms of expression. There is a tendency, due to colours and qualities of glaze, to subdue extremes of form to a common level.
9. Traditionally, this type of glaze is applied by pouring or dipping. There is, however, no reason why it should not be applied by other means, such as spraying, as long as the correct thickness of glaze is achieved.
10. Double-glazing techniques can give very rich and interesting results.

OXIDIZED-STONEWARE GLAZES 1,150°C. TO 1,250°C.

Main points of interest

1. Colour and quality may range from that found in some earthenware glazes to those found in reduced-stoneware glazes.

2. In many ways oxidized glazes have similar points to those mentioned under reduced-stoneware glazes.

Firing glazed tilework

The main requirements for firing glazed tiles are the same as for firing any other pottery ware, with the following special suggestions:

1. Tiles are very easily packed into kilns if the proper kiln furniture is used. This often leads to the temptation to overpack a kiln. When electric kilns are used, tiles should be set with a gap of at least $1\frac{1}{2}$ in. between the elements and their edges. In flame-fired kilns precautions should be taken to exclude the possibility of uneven firing across the tiles' area.

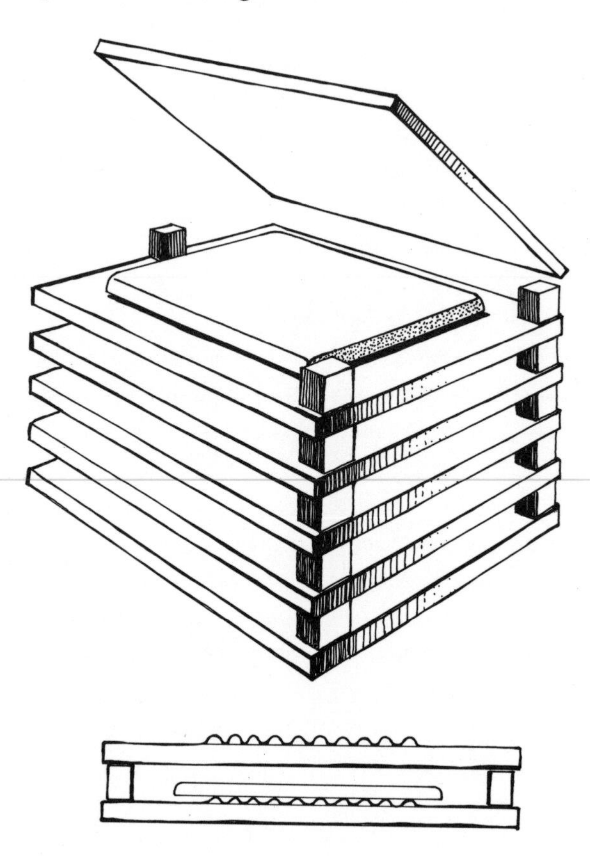

Fig. 28. The use of tile bats

2. When special kiln furniture is used (tile bats) to set tiles, care must be taken that enough space is left between the bottom of the tile bats and the top of the tile, to allow expansion or bubbling of glaze to take place without contact with the tile bat (Fig. 28).
3. Any glaze that may accidentally be on the underside of the tile must be sponged off to avoid sticking the tile to the kiln furniture when fired.
4. Any identification numbers, on the back of the tiles, should be painted in a metallic oxide, e.g. FeO., and never in glaze material.
5. A kiln that is fully packed with tiles can often change its firing characteristics, which may result in uneven temperatures. Note should be taken of any uneven firing and rectified in the usual ways:
   (a) Altering the pattern for setting the ware.
   (b) Changing the firing cycle.
   (c) Soaking for a length of time at maximum desired temperature.
6. When firing commercially-made tiles, ensure that the initial heating period is slow and even.
7. When packing re-glazed commercial tiles, the fingers may disturb the glaze around the edges of the tile. This may be overcome by adding gum arabic to the glaze before use.

Kiln furniture

There are many special designs for tile bats; some may be excluded from general use due to their specialization.

The most useful bat is the one which will accommodate both 6 in. × 6 in. and $4\frac{1}{4}$ in. × $4\frac{1}{4}$ in. sq. tiles. Any tiles larger than these measurements may be accommodated on existing kiln furniture designed for general use.

Whenever possible, avoid firing tiles in any other position than the horizontal. Laying the tile flat in glaze firings ensures that no distortion of the design occurs through the glaze running over the surface. Some tile bats have small raised dots over their surface. These will prove to be useful in stopping the tile sticking to the bat, should excess glaze be present. If the tile bat does not have raised dots, it should be given a light coating of bat wash to prevent glaze sticking to its surface. If this is done, care must be taken to avoid accidentally brushing bat wash on to the tile's surface when packing the kiln. A check should be made that no loose particles of dust or ceramic materials are adhering to the underside of the bats. 'Bat wash' may be made by mixing 50 per cent flint and 50 per cent china clay with water.

Tiles packed on to bats may be stacked to almost any height as long as the building of the column of bats is regular and done with care. The most efficient propping system for tile bats is one of supporting the bats in three places—at two corners and in the centre of the opposite side (Fig. 28).

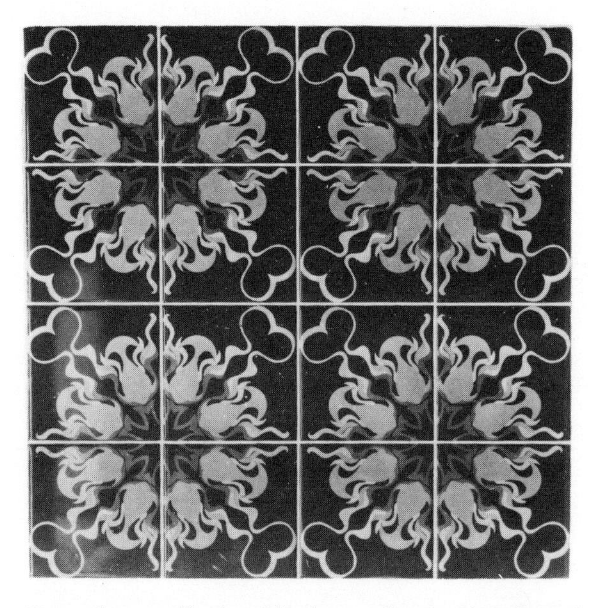

Repeating motif printed in three colours on a coloured glazed tile. Designed and printed by Jenny Williamson, A.T.D., Loughborough College of Art

6 · On-glaze and Underglaze Decoration

On-glaze decoration

This technique may be considered as being divided into two main areas.

1. The application of colours to a *fired* glaze surface.
2. The application of colours to an *unfired* glaze surface.

The basic difference in these two areas which is of interest to the tile decorator is as follows:

Designs applied to a fired glaze surface may be wiped away with little loss of time, labour or materials. When designs that are applied to unfired glaze surfaces are erased, the raw glaze surface is destroyed and more time, labour and material is wasted. This fact often creates inhibitions in the mind of the decorator when unfired glaze surfaces are in use. At the present time the use of unfired glaze surfaces as areas for decoration is in a decline and the more controlled, less hazardous, enamels on fired glaze technique is being used more and more.

It is not the lack of ideas or creativity that brings this situation about; in industrial situations it is the need for speed and efficiency; in studio situations I believe it to be the already mentioned inhibitions.

The solution to this problem lies in the familiarity that one may achieve with techniques.

To prove the usefulness of painting designs on unfired glaze, we have only to refer to the Delft tilework of the seventeenth and eighteenth centuries, where we may see rich colours and textures; bold designs carried out with spontaneity and certainty, ranging in content from the primitive to the sophisticated.

On-glaze materials and methods of application to 'fired' glaze surfaces

Enamels 700°C. to 800°C.

Enamels are usually purchased ready-made from suppliers of ceramic materials.

The colour range of enamels is almost unlimited and many manufacturers will mix colours to match customers' requirements.

Enamels may be purchased in a powder form or ready mixed with either a painting medium or a silk-screening medium. Colours should not be intermixed except under the manufacturers' instructions.

The quality of fired enamels may be likened to that of household gloss paint, tending as it does to sit on the glaze's surface, giving a dense, opaque colour with strong edge definition.

The colour of the raw enamel will often closely represent the colour achieved after firing. This fact will be helpful in deciding the colour relationships when the work is in progress.

Enamels should only be applied to fired glaze surfaces. The glaze used as a base may be of any temperature range and may be of any colour and surface quality (matt, gloss). With glazes that have been fired at temperatures up to 1,100°C. the enamels should be fired at between 700°C.–750°C. If the base glaze is fired above 1,100°C. and up to 1,300°C. the firing temperature for the enamels should be increased 750°C.–800°C. This allows the enamel to fix itself firmly to the glaze's surface.

Enamels may be applied to the tile's surface in any one or in any combination of the following techniques:

1. Brush painting.
2. Spraying, stencilled or stippled.
3. Screen printing.
4. Decalcomania transfers.
5. Lithography.
6. Groundlaying.
7. Stamping.

PAINTED ENAMELS

Traditional techniques for painting enamels require a range of specially shaped brushes. These brushes were developed to fulfil the stylistic and technical requirements existing at any one time in the decorator's art. There is therefore no need to use any of these traditional brushes; any brush will suffice that fulfils the requirements placed on it.

Painted enamels invariably show the mark of the brush after they have been fired. It is this fact that has been recognized and utilized in nearly all historical examples of this type of work. Although there is no reason why designs should not be painted by other means, it is still true to say that the brush marks will contribute an effect to the finished work and the success of the design often depends on the way these marks work with or against the finished effect. The same attitude may be applied to the medium used for painting. The traditional medium is a mixture of fat oil and turpentine which gives an excellent fluid for smooth painting. It may, however, be found convenient and productive to use other media. Experiments in this direction will show the variations that may be achieved with different painting fluids. One example which may be useful to employ is ready-mixed silk-screening enamel.

In addition to being used by themselves for their inherent qualities, painted enamels may be used to put the finishing touches or details to a design, carried out by other techniques. In this way they may contribute in a positive way, qualities and colour predetermined at the designing stage, or they may help in correcting accidents or mistakes. Painted enamels may be used for any work, lying between the demands of simple patterns and the complications in painted representations of natural objects or scenes etc.

SPRAYED, STENCILLED OR STIPPLED ENAMELS

Enamels may be applied to a tile's surface by spraying or stencilling in broad areas, either as an end in itself or as preparation for some other technique, sgraffito, etc.

Any of these methods may be used to create textures, ranging from the finest hazy qualities gained by spraying, to the coarser qualities produced by stippling with an open textured sponge or even a piece of newspaper screwed into a ball.

Stencilled enamels may be used in exactly the same way as one would stencil poster paints on paper. The success of such work depends on the accuracy with which the stencil is cut and the efficiency with which the colour is applied.

Spraying, stencilling and stippling may be carried out on decalcomania paper and then transferred to the tile's surface. Designs which have the qualities of cut paper may be made in this way.

Flat areas of colour may be applied to the decalcomania paper or textures and patterns placed on its surface. When these have dried, shapes may be cut from the sheet of transfer paper and applied to the tile.

The best medium to use with the enamel for this technique is silk-screening medium, as it dries to a strong skin over the transfer paper's surface and does not move about whilst the paper is being wetted prior to transference.

Sprayed or aerographed enamels can create broad expanses of colour or subtle modelling of shapes. The success of such work depends upon the preparation of the enamel colour and its mixing with the spraying medium.

The enamel colour used for this operation must be ground to a finer particle size than exists in its normal use. Specially prepared enamels may be purchased for this purpose. For general work it will be found that hand grinding the enamel and medium in a mortar and pestle, followed by screening through a fine sieve, will give satisfactory results. The medium used may be a very thin fluid made from fat oil and turpentine or even silk-screening medium thinned to allow its movement through the spray gun. Experimentation will show results from various media.

SILK-SCREENING ENAMELS

This technique is fully dealt with in Chapter 7 which covers both direct and transfer printing.

LITHOGRAPHY

This technique is usually out of the reach of small studio potters, requiring as it does special printing equipment. Generally speaking, this technique has been superseded in industry by silk-screening. Further reference may be made to the problems and uses of lithography in, for example, *Ceramic Colours and Pottery Decoration*, by Kenneth Shaw, listed in the bibliography.

GROUNDLAYING ENAMELS

This technique may be employed when a tile's surface is to be completely covered by an even coating of enamel colour.

The tile's surface is painted with 'groundlaying' oil. After this oil has dried to a tacky state, the brush marks are obliterated by tamping or 'bossing' over the surface with a pad made by wrapping a ball of cotton wool in a piece of silk. The 'bossing' is continued until the oil is perfectly even over the tile's surface.

Powdered enamel colour is now sprinkled over the oiled surface by means of a pad of cotton wool. Care must be taken that the woollen pad does not touch the surface of the oil. If this happens, the resulting smudge will invariably show after the colour is fired.

Once the colour is uniformly dispersed over the oiled surface the tile may be fired.

Groundlaying is a useful method of preparing a coloured background for sgraffito work. The difficulty with this technique is found in the skill necessary to 'boss' the oil evenly and to disperse the enamel colour consistently over the tile's surface.

STAMPING ENAMELS

This technique is carried out with enamel colour that has been mixed with 'Stamping Oil' and applied to the tile's surface with a rubber stamp mounted on a thin cushion of foam rubber (Fig. 29).

The rubber stamp is made to the shape of the design by casting or cutting.

The colour is prepared by thoroughly mixing with palette and palette knife, after which it is spread thinly and evenly over a smooth base, such as a spare tile.

The rubber stamp is pressed on to this colour and then transferred to the surface to be decorated.

Designs made in this way should not be too large. The most successful application for this technique is probably that of creating designs that are composed of small repeated motives (Fig. 29).

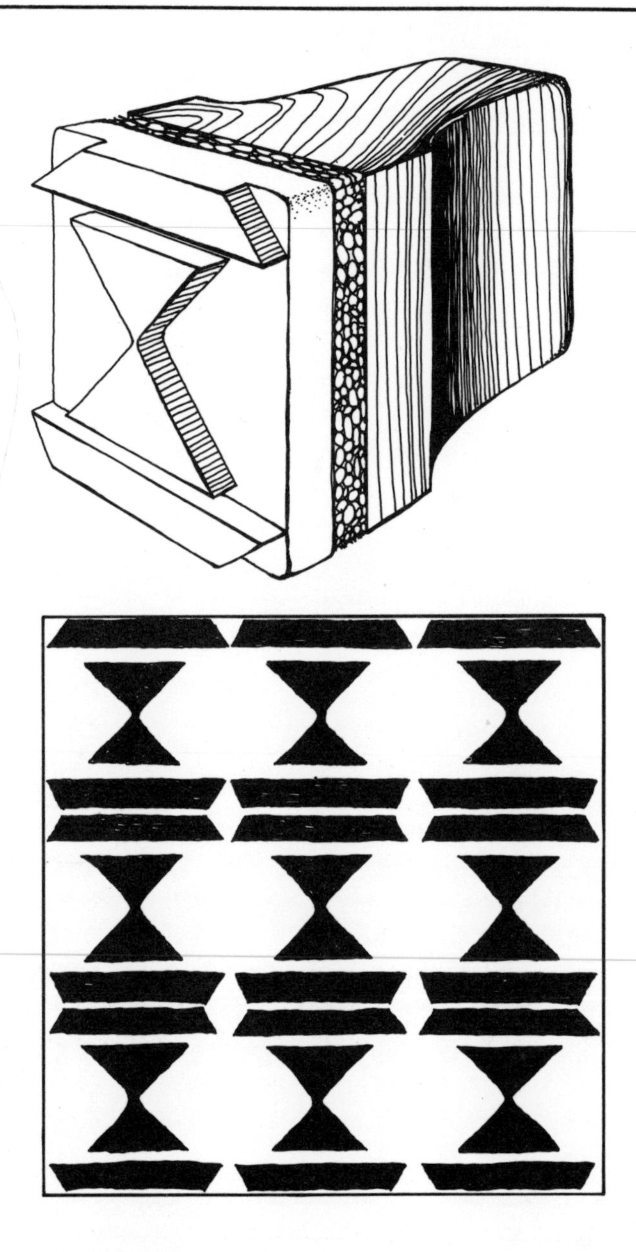

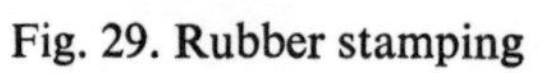

Fig. 29. Rubber stamping

METALLIC LUSTRES

These may be considered as an extension of enamel colours. In the main, they may be applied by all techniques suitable for enamels and are fired to the tile's surface at approximately the same temperatures as are enamels.

For the successful use of metallic lustres, it is absolutely essential to follow the manufacturers' recommendations for use.

'PIGMENTS' 700°C. TO 1,300°C.

Pigments are the metallic oxides that form the basis for all other ceramic colours. These pigments may be used in their raw state to create colour and surface qualities. They may be used singly or in combination one with another.

The ones most used in small pottery studios are as follows:

Metallic oxide	*Colour when fired*
Copper carbonate	Green
Cobalt carbonate	Blue
Iron oxide	Red/Brown
Chromium oxide	Dark Green
Manganese oxide	Dark Brown
Tin oxide	White

The development of the colours mentioned above depends on the situation in which the pigments are used. If the pigments are simply painted on the glaze surface, the result is generally a black or a dark brown colour. With the exceptions of tin oxide and chromium oxide, which give white and dark green.

To realize their full colour potential, the pigments have either to be mixed with other materials and so disperse their concentration, or they have to be applied thinly over a glaze which will allow their colour to show. This does not, however, exclude their single use and the subsequent production after firing of dark browns and blacks.

An example of a pigment which gives a dark brown colour, and which has a green 'halo' effect at the edges of the design, is as follows:

Recipe for pigment to use with earthenware base glazes:

2 parts copper carbonate
3 parts iron oxide
1 part transparent glaze or frit.

The component parts of this pigment are simply mixed together with water and screened through a 180-size sieve. Alternatively, they may be mixed with screening medium and screen printed. The copper in this recipe produces the green 'halo', the iron in conjunction with the copper produces the dark brown. The glaze or frit fluxes the two oxides together and ensures that they stick to the surface of the base glaze. The green 'halo' effect is produced by the dispersion of copper carbonate at the edges of the design. This pigment works best on an opaque white base glaze.

It will be seen from this one example that the fired colour of the pigment depends on its concentration, the glaze over which it is painted and the other ingredients (if any) in the mixture.

The qualities gained from pigments are linked to those techniques and styles of design associated with 'hand decoration'. This is due in part to traditional uses of pigments and their inherent 'earthy' qualities.

On-glaze decoration to 'unfired' glaze surfaces

This technique is traditionally referred to as delft, faience or majolica painting. These names are associations with the historical and geographical centres of production of this work. They all mean the same thing—applying colour to create a design on the surface of a glaze before that glaze is fired.

The process is as follows:

1. The tile's surface is covered by the base glaze. This may be done by spraying or pouring the glaze. The tile used may be biscuit or may be a ready-fired glazed tile. If the tile is biscuit, little difficulty will be found in applying the glaze. The porous nature of the biscuit clay will hold the glaze in position. If, however, glazed tiles are used, it may be found necessary to use the glaze to be applied in a thicker consistency than is normal. It will be found an advantage in both cases to add a small amount of gum arabic to the glaze before application. (One tablespoon of gum to one pint glaze.) This

gum will help the glaze retain its position after drying and when decoration is commenced.

2. The traditional colours used for on-glaze painting are normally purchased ready-made. There is, however, no reason why pigments or basic metallic oxides should not be used in this work, or even mixed with ready-made colours. These colours are prepared by grinding on a palette with a palette knife. The medium used is water plus a small amount of gum arabic to help fix the powdery colour when dry and prevent smudging. If too much gum arabic is used in the preparation of colours, they will have the tendency to flake off the tile's surface when dry. It will be found an advantage to add a little of the base glaze to the colour; using too much must be guarded against. One or two brushfuls should be sufficient. The addition of this glaze will help in fluxing the colour to the tile's surface when it is fired.
3. When biscuit tiles are used, the colour applied should be mixed to a thinner consistency than at first thought correct. This is due to the absorbency of the tile and glaze. When the colour is applied, there will be a tendency for the glazed surface to suck the colour from the brush and this often leads to too thick a deposit which when fired, will not flux smoothly into the glaze surface.
4. If overpainting of one colour by another is desired, care should be taken that the under colour is not smudged by the second application of colour. The addition of gum arabic to the colour will help overcome this problem.
5. It is sometimes the practice to spray a very light coating of a transparent glaze over the finished painted work. This is done to ensure that the whole surface of the design is glossy and helps overcome any mistakes made in the thickness of the applied colour, which can result, after firing, in patches of the design remaining powdery or pitted with the bubbling that sometimes takes place with excess colour.

Decoration of raw, unfired glaze surfaces may be carried out in techniques other than the traditional brush painting. Spraying, stencilling and stippling are all possible. The same rules apply to these techniques as apply for brush painting. Further to this, the marks left by any tool used for applying the colour will show after firing (as with enamels). This effect has to be taken into account when designing with this technique.

The silk-screen process may be applied to raw glaze decorating with the following provisions:

1. The glaze must be hardened on to the surface of the tile by firing at approximately 700°C.–800°C. This will prevent the glaze being lifted off the tile's surface by the sticky nature of screening medium.
2. An alternative to direct screening is to print the design on tissue paper and immediately press this down on to the fire-hardened glaze. Some details may be lost in this way and generally speaking only the strongest colours should be used in this manner. This technique is particularly useful when decorating a tile with a modelled surface.

Decorating an *unfired* glaze surface may be performed on tiles to be fired at any temperature.

The basic techniques are the same for earthenware and stoneware.

Differences appear in the suitability of some of the ready-made colours. Before using any purchased on-glaze colour, check its firing range with the manufacturer. There are colours designed to be used at both low and high temperatures—providing the atmosphere in the kiln is oxidizing.

If on-glaze decoration is to be applied to reduced-stoneware tiles, the materials will be confined to pigments or base metallic oxides, but most of these may be applied with techniques already described.

7 · Silk-screen Printing

This technique is an extension of simple stencilling, where the stencil is supported by the mesh of a fabric stretched tightly across a wooden frame. Stencil, fabric and wooden frame make the printing screen. The screen is held over the surface on which the design is to be printed and ceramic ink is forced through the mesh openings left in the fabric by the areas of the design (Fig. 30a).

Silk-screen printing is at the same time easy to master and versatile in its application. As a ceramic decorating technique it is used by studio potters and large tile manufacturing companies.

Excellent results may be achieved with the simplest of apparatus, much of which may be made by oneself, without having to invest large sums of money in sophisticated machinery.

Almost any type of design may be executed by the screen method. The main requirement that the design must fulfil, is that it should be capable of being expressed in terms of black and white or positive and negative. Tonal effects are achieved by using graded textures (Fig. 31).

Basic silk-screening equipment:

1. Screen fabric—silk, nylon, organdie.
2. Wooden frames with inside measurements exceeding the dimensions of the design by at least 2 in. all round.
3. Printing baseboard with hinge assembly to carry wooden frame—vacuum or non-vacuum.
4. Stencil materials—cut paper, cut film, photographic stencil.
5. Medium for ceramic inks and/or ready-mixed ceramic inks.
6. Rubber or plastic squeegee.
7. Exposing lamp, if photographic stencil is used.
8. Turpentine substitute, cleaning rags, palette knife, gummed brown paper strip.

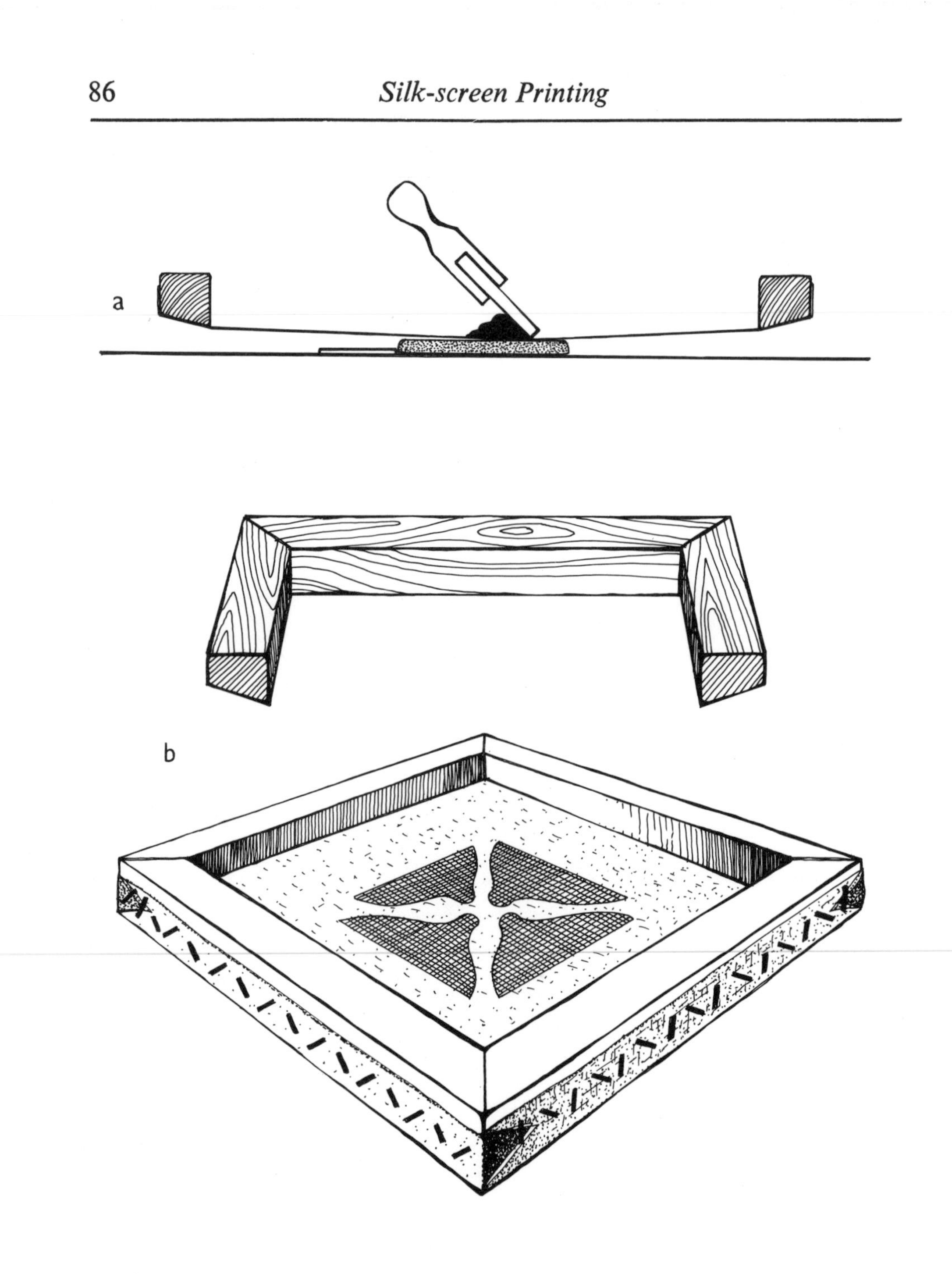

Fig. 30. The silk-screening frame

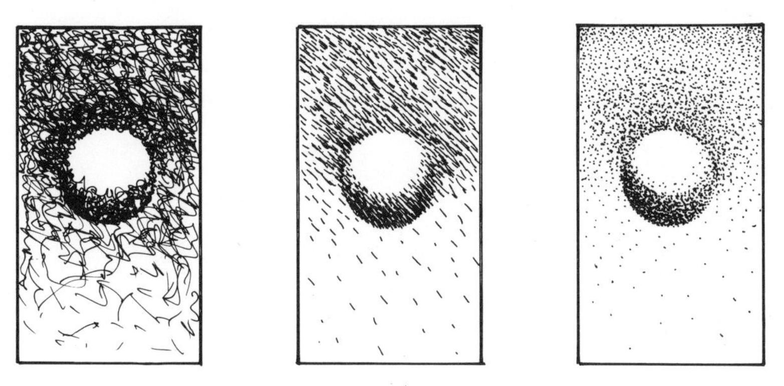

Fig. 31. Tonal effects using black and white textures

9. Water soluble screen stopper (Blue Stopper).
10. Staple gun.

Silk-screen fabrics

As the name suggests, silk may be used as a printing fabric; alternatives are nylon and other manmade fibres. The cheapest, but not perhaps the most efficient fabric is organdie. These fabrics are made in different grades with varying sizes of mesh. The use of the correct-size mesh is important if good-quality prints are to be made. The choice of mesh size depends on the ceramic ink—enamel, glaze or pigment—and the type of stencil used to form the design. Enamel printing requires a fine-mesh fabric which will give the thin layer of colour and the sharp edge definition associated with enamels. Printing with glaze materials demands a coarse-mesh fabric to allow the large glaze particles to pass through the screen. The coarse mesh will also permit a heavy deposit of colour and allows the true nature of the glaze to mature when fired.

The way in which stencil and fabric function in printing may be seen in Fig. 30 (a).

The most useful fabric is nylon, which if properly prepared and carefully handled, may be used time and time again without loss of printing quality.

Wooden printing frames

These frames may be made from well-seasoned hard or soft woods.

The inside measurements of the frame should always exceed the size of the printed design by at least 2 in. This allows room for the squeegee to travel freely and provides an area inside the screen in which a reservoir of ceramic ink may be contained, without overlapping the open mesh of the design (Fig. 30b).

The frame should be made from wood having a sectional dimension of at least 2 in. × $1\frac{1}{2}$ in. The shape of the section may be rectangular, although there is some advantage in having one side bevelled. This bevel helps in tightening the fabric when it is being fixed to the frame. The bevel will also prevent printing ink from leaking outwards at the point at which fabric and frame touch (Fig. 30b).

The construction of frames may be carried out using one of the following corner joints. There is little to be gained by using any one of these joints and the choice of which to use depends on the facilities available for their construction.

1. *Mitre, nails and glue* (Fig. 32a)

Each side of the frame is cut with 45° mitre joints. Glue and nail each corner, one after another, holding each with a vice when nailing. The frame may be held together before nailing and after gluing by tying round with a strong cord. The cord may be tightened by forcing small blocks of wood between it and the frame (Fig. 33).

2. *Square, overlapping joints* (Fig. 32b)

This method should not be used if the sides of the frame are to be bevelled.

3. *Butt joints held together with metal brackets* (Fig. 32c)

This is the simplest joint to make but its success depends on the size and strength of the metal brackets. The sides may be bevelled after the frame has been screwed together.

The mitred joint is the best to use as it ensures that the frame may be flat and strong. Other methods of joining, such as dovetailing, may be used but depend on the skill of the woodworker for their success.

When made, the frame should be finished by painting its entire surface with

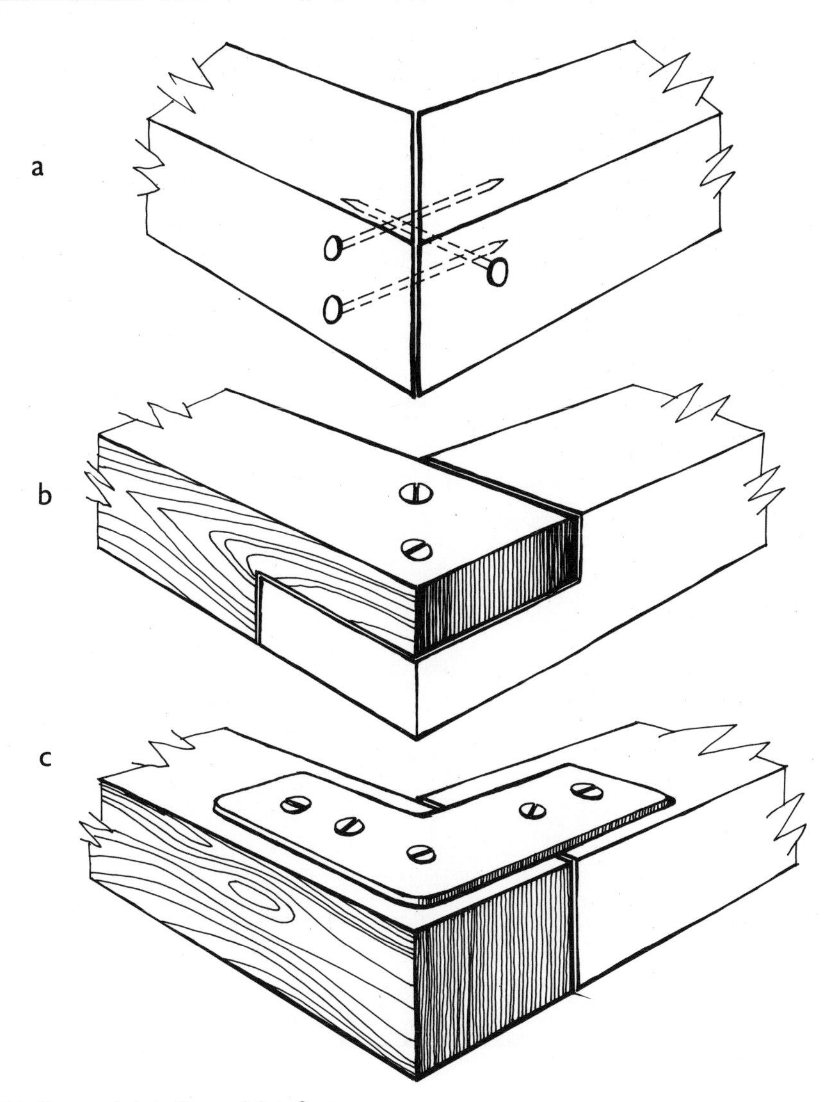

Fig. 32. Corner joints for making frames

a wood sealant. This will prevent the absorption of water when the screen is washed and reclaimed.

All corners and edges of the wooden frame should be sanded round and smooth. This will prevent tearing the fabric accidentally when it is being stretched over the frame.

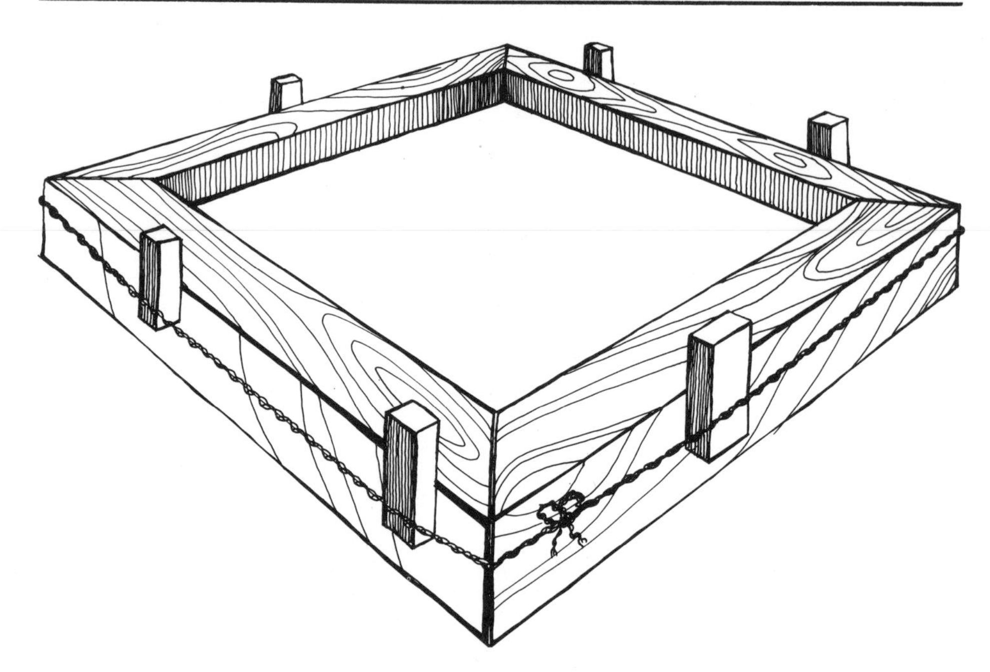

Fig. 33. Tying the frame when gluing and nailing

Preparing the screen

The fabric should be stretched as tightly and as evenly as possible across the area outlined by the frame. Any folds or undulations across the fabric will cause faults in the application of the stencil and in the printing.

The fabric should be fixed to the frame in the following manner:

1. Cut a piece of fabric 2 in. larger in size, on all sides, than the measurements of the wooden frame (Fig. 34a).
2. Fold the edges of the fabric lengthways in two halves in folds (Fig. 34b). These folds strengthen the fabric and prevent tearing when the fabric is stapled.
3. Staple the fabric to the frame at the centre point of each side, pulling the fabric tight after each staple (Fig. 34c).
4. Repeat the stapling, working outwards from the centre to the corners of the frame. Stapling the fabric on opposite sides as one works around the frame (Fig. 34d). The gap between staples should be approximately $\frac{1}{2}$ in.
5. The last staples should fix down any loose fabric at the corners, which should be pulled tight diagonally across the frame (Fig. 34e).

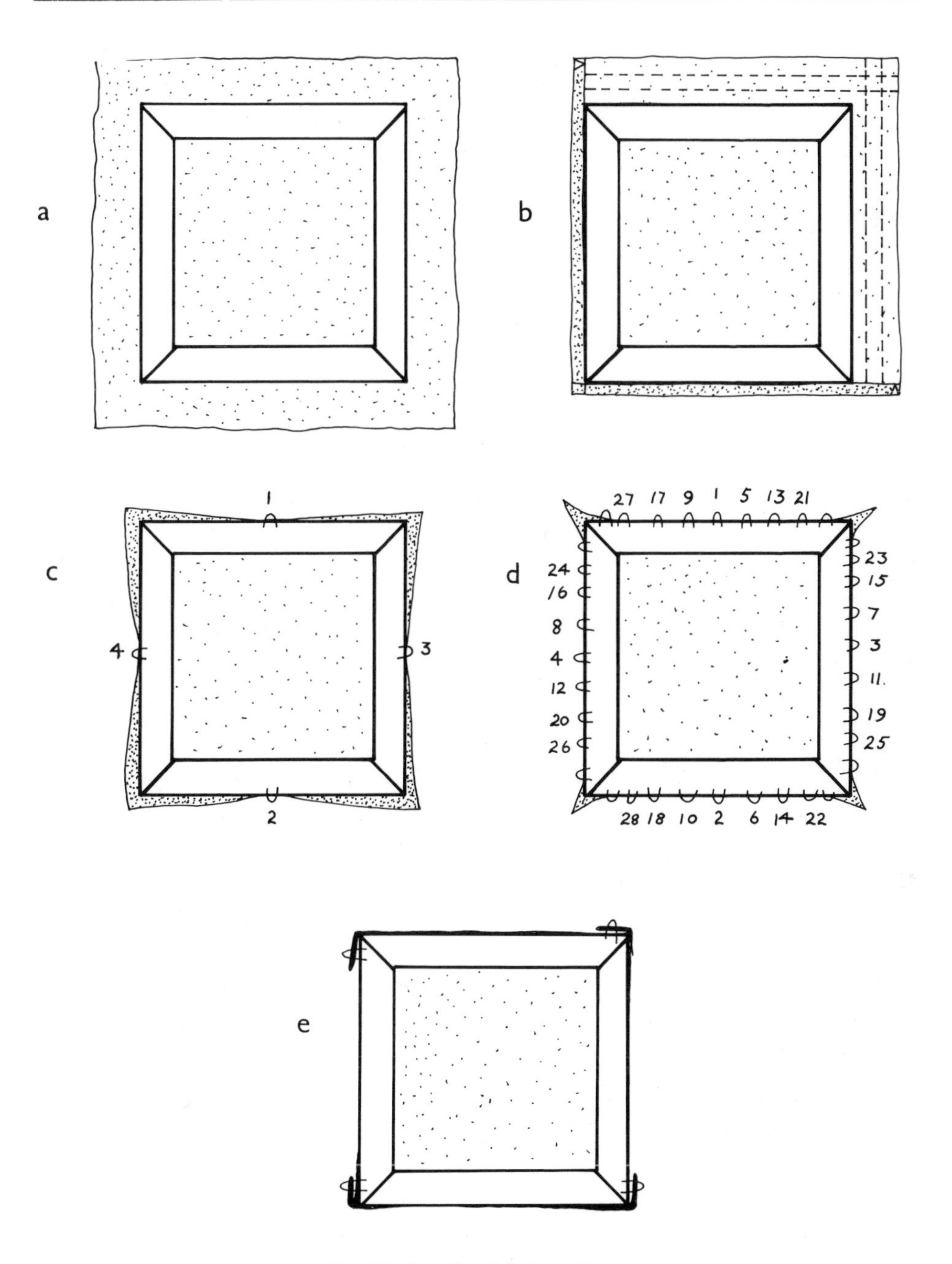

Fig. 34. Stapling fabric to frame

6. Check fabric for any loose parts. These may be pulled tight and stapled firm.
7. The screen should now be washed to clear away any dirt or grease on the mesh. After washing and drying the screen is ready for use.

The printing baseboard

This baseboard holds the screen and the tile in position whilst printing takes place.

Baseboards may be quite simple structures consisting of a flat board with raised hinges at one end (Fig. 35), or they may be more complex affairs which enable the operator to adjust the height of the screen above the printing surface and the horizontal position of the screen for accurate registration of multi-colour printing. Further refinements are counterbalance weights to keep the screen in a raised position when removing the tile after printing and a vacuum bed to retain decalcomania paper in position when transfers are printed. Neither of these two refinements help the quality of the print, but they do enable the work to be done with more speed and efficiency, especially when long runs of printing are undertaken.

A simple baseboard to print single tiles or small panels of tiles would be made in the following manner:

1. A piece of 1 in. thick blockboard is cut to size—approximately 2 ft. sq. The edges of this board should be sanded smooth and its entire surface painted with a wood sealant.
2. A length of wood 2 in. wide and $\frac{1}{4}$ in. thicker than the depth of screen used for printing is screwed down along one edge of the blockboard. Alternatively the length of wood may be secured to the baseboard with adjusting bolts. These bolts allow the screen to be lifted to various heights (Fig. 36), allowing all thicknesses of tile to be used in direct printing, and transfer paper to be printed with the screen fully lowered.
3. Two hinges of at least 2 in. in length and preferably made of brass, are screwed one at each end of the piece of wood (Fig. 35). These hinges provide points at which the screen may be fixed to the baseboard and the means by which the screen is raised and lowered when printing is commenced.
4. A propping arm may be attached to the screen before printing begins. This arm allows the screen to be left in a raised position between prints, freeing

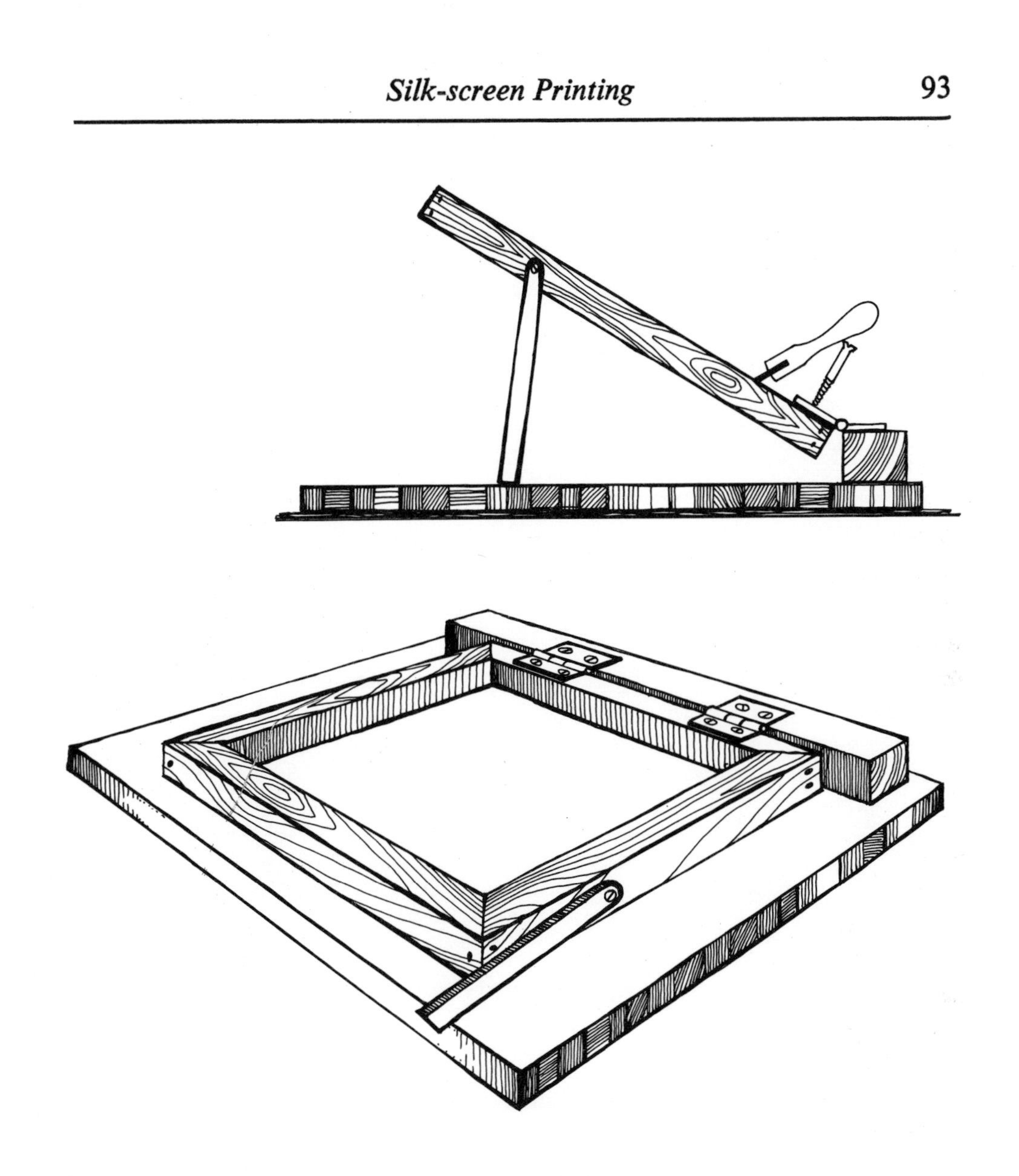

Fig. 35. A simple wooden baseboard for screen printing

both hands for removing the printed tile and replacing with the next tile to be printed. It will be found an extra advantage to have a large screw projecting vertically from the back edge of the screen. This will support the squeegee whilst the tile is removed and replaced (Fig. 35).

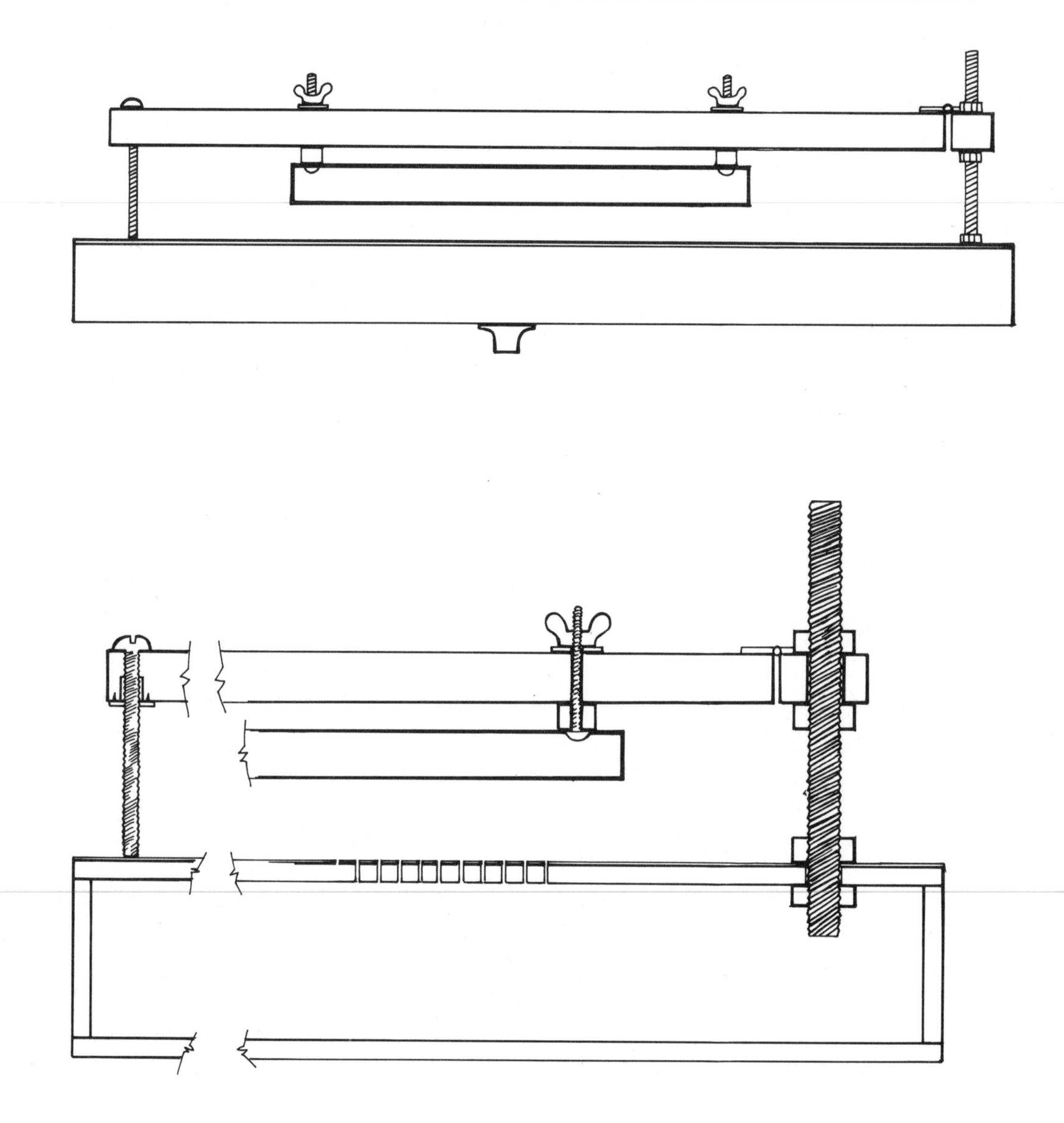

Fig. 36. Bolt adjustments on a vacuum base for screen printing

Adjustable and vacuum bed baseboard

The usefulness of the printing base is greatly increased if it is fitted with an adjustable hinge assembly and a vacuum bed.

The adjustable hinges enable multicoloured prints to be taken with accuracy of registration and they also allow different thicknesses of tile to be printed together with decalcomania transfer paper.

Transfers may be printed on a non-vacuum base but some means by which the paper may be held securely in position must be used. This usually entails Sellotape at the corners of the sheet of transfer paper and tends to be an untidy technique, especially if colour registration is necessary. It is therefore preferable to print transfers on a base equipped with a vacuum. An ordinary vacuum cleaner may be utilized and the base should be modified as follows (Figs. 36 and 37):

1. An airtight box is made from wood 4 or 5 in. deep with the horizontal measurements being of a size to cater for the maximum printed area required.
2. The top of this basebox should be covered with a sheet of plastic laminate and glued firmly in position with impact adhesive.
3. $\frac{1}{16}$ in. diameter holes should be drilled through both wood and laminate. These holes should be spaced at $\frac{1}{2}$ in. intervals over the maximum printing area required.
4. A vacuum cleaner is connected underneath or to one side of the box.
5. An on/off switch should be placed near at hand to control the vacuum cleaner—switching on for printing and off when the printed transfer is removed.

Stencil materials

The choice of stencil depends on the content of the design and the thickness and quality required for the print.

CUT-PAPER STENCILS

Paper stencils are the simplest to make but they have disadvantages in use. They have a very short printing life and tend to smudge designs. They should

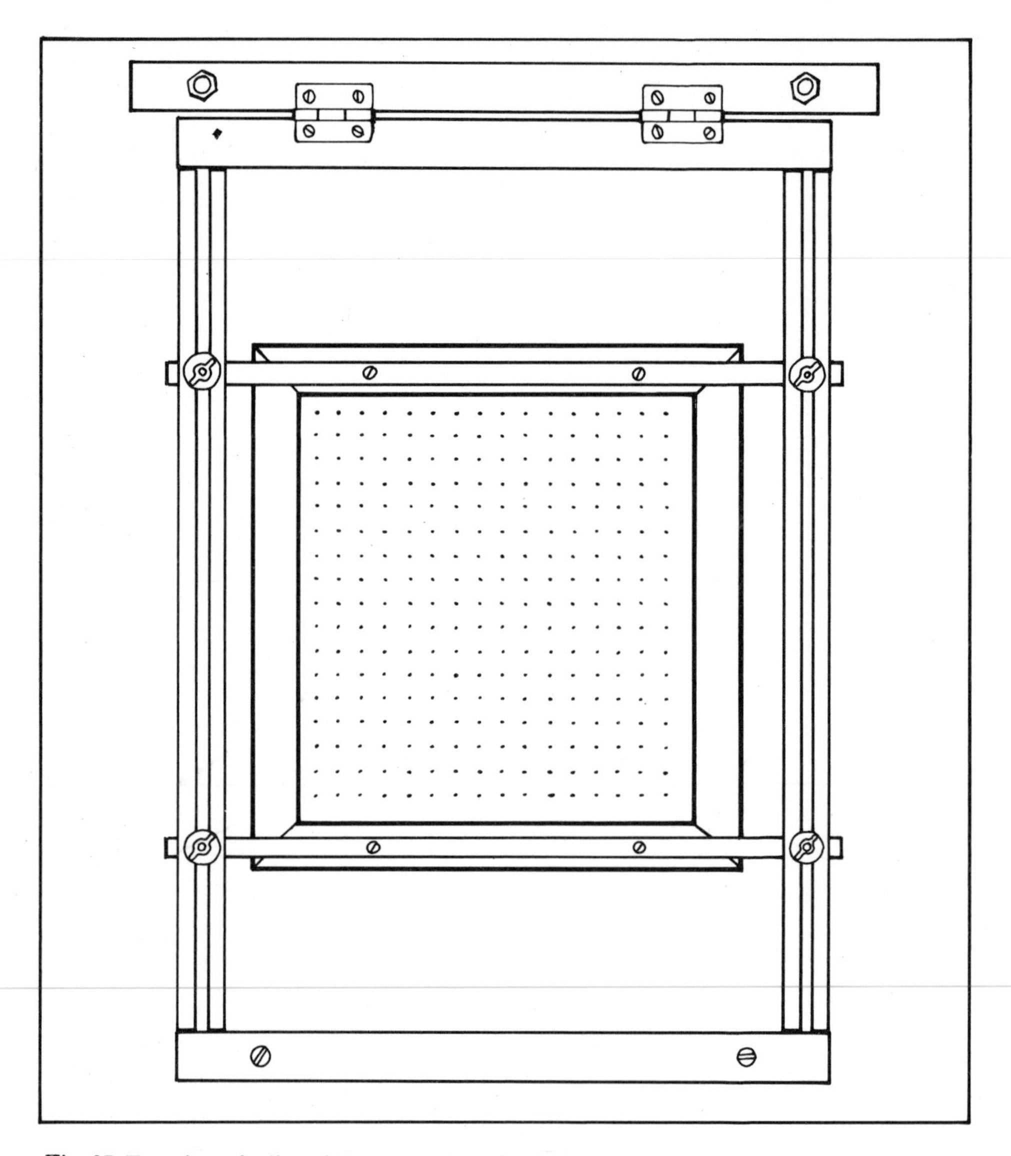

Fig. 37. Top view of adjustable vacuum base for screen printing

only be used for printing designs composed of large areas of simple shapes and are not suitable for complex or detailed designs.

Some difficulty may be experienced in applying the stencil to the screen fabric. Paper stencils are, however, a direct introduction to silk-screen processes and allow initial experiments to take place with the minimum of preparation.

METHOD FOR CUT-PAPER STENCILS

Almost any paper will make a stencil; thin cartridge paper being, perhaps, the most useful.

Cut the design from the centre of a piece of paper that is large enough to cover the whole surface of the screen. The design may be cut from the paper with a sharp craft knife or razor blade.

Apply a water-based glue over the back surface of the cut stencil. Lay prepared screen on to the glued side of a stencil and press down firmly, ensuring even adhesion, with special attention to the edges of the design. Wipe away any glue that may have run out from under the stencil and over the design. This may be done from inside the screen using a damp cloth. Block out any parts of the mesh left open with screen stopper, except the area making the design.

When screen stopper and glue are perfectly dry, the inside corners of the screen are blocked out with gummed paper strip. After the gummed paper strip has dried, the screen is ready for printing.

CUT-FILM STENCILS

These stencils are specially prepared and consist of a shellac or fish glue stencil material supported by a paper backing.

The design to be printed is cut lightly through the stencil material, which may then be peeled away. The areas of stencil material removed equal the design to be printed. When the cutting is complete, the stencil is pressed on to the fabric of the screen with a hot iron.

Cut-film stencils have the advantage over paper stencils of withstanding prolonged printing runs. The paper backing on these stencils will allow more complex designs to be cut than those gained when using paper stencils. 'Blue film' and 'Green film' are two types of cut-film stencils most suited to ceramic inks. They are both soluble in water and will withstand the oil medium used for printing and the turpentine used for cleaning the screen.

CUTTING AND APPLYING THE FILM

1. Use a piece of film at least 1 in. larger all round than the design to be printed.

2. Place the film over a master drawing of the design and hold in position with tape. The stencil material must be placed uppermost to allow cutting to take place.
3. Cut lightly through the stencil material following the master drawing. Do not cut too deeply; this may result in spoiling the film by cutting through the backing paper. The correct cutting pressure may be found by experimenting on a spare piece of film.
4. Peel off the areas of the stencil material that equal the design. Check before removing these areas that the cutting is complete and the piece to be taken away is free on all sides and especially at sharp corners.
5. After all areas of design have been removed, place the film, stencil side uppermost, on a stiff and flat piece of card. This card will act as a support when the ironing-on process begins.
6. When either 'Blue film' or 'Green film' is ironed on to a screen it is necessary to dampen the fabric of the screen. This is carried out after the screen has been washed and thoroughly dried.

   Saturate a piece of lint-free cloth with water. Wring out the water until the cloth is 'wet-damp'. Rub the damp cloth over the fabric until it can be seen that the mesh of the fabric is holding an even film of moisture.
7. Lay damp screen over cut film which is laying on flat card backing. Place a piece of newspaper inside the screen, covering the whole of the cut film's area.
8. The film is now ready to be ironed on to the screen. An ordinary domestic iron with a heat control is suitable.

   The temperature of the iron should be set for the type of material used in making the screen. Press firmly down on the newspaper inside the screen, keeping the iron moving at all times. As the ironing progresses, the cut-film stencil will adhere to the mesh of the screen. The correct amount of ironing may be judged by the slight colour change that takes place in the stencil, as seen through the fabric. The ironing should continue until the colour change is equal over the entire surface of the stencil.

   Too much ironing or too high a temperature will result in the stencil losing its adhesion and so it is best to experiment before using this technique on an actual piece of work.
9. After ironing is complete, the backing paper supporting the stencil material may be peeled away. This should be done slowly, noting if any parts of

the stencil are being taken away. If any stencil does move with the backing paper, further ironing at that point is necessary.

10. The screen is now finished in the way described for cut-paper stencils—with screen stopper and gummed-paper strip.

Photographic stencils

These stencils fall into two main categories:

1. Where the stencil material is light sensitized by oneself, prior to use, as with gelatine dichromate.
2. Ready sensitized stencils such as 'Autotype 5-Star Film'.

The use of 'Autotype 5-Star Film' precludes some preparation and if the manufacturers' instructions are followed, this film will be found to be the most direct and simple photographic technique to use. For this reason only the 5-Star film method is described in this chapter. If for any reason other techniques are necessary, the procedures in them are virtually identical for ceramic printing as for any other printing materials and reference may be made to specialized publications on silk-screen techniques.

BASIC OUTLINE FOR USING 5-STAR FILM

1. The design is drawn or painted in an opaque paint or ink on the surface of a transparent film, e.g. 'Kodatrace'. Alternatively the design, if suitable, may be cut from opaque paper. Designs may also be made from photographs using 'line film' such as Ilford's 'Formolith' or Kodak's 'Kodalith'. These line films are used to make a positive transparency from a photographic negative.
2. The design in the form of a positive transparency is laid over the 5-Star film and exposed to light.
3. The 5-Star film is 'fixed' in a bath of hydrogen peroxide and then washed in warm water to reveal the design.
4. The film is pressed on the screen and the supporting material removed.

If the manufacturers' instructions are followed, the 5-Star film technique is as simple as outlined above. The procedure is the same for all types of design and results are consistent. The important part of this technique is the preparation of the positive transparency. There are many ways in which this transparency may be treated, some of which are outlined below:

Painted designs

Designs may be painted on the surface of transparent acetate film, e.g. 'Kodatrace'.

Any paint may be used, providing that it is completely opaque to light when dry. Photographic retouching paint is normally used and is similar to poster paints in its application.

If possible, it is best to do all the painting over a light box as shown in Fig. 38. If a light box is not at hand, the design must be held up to a strong light from time to time, in order that complete opacity may be achieved.

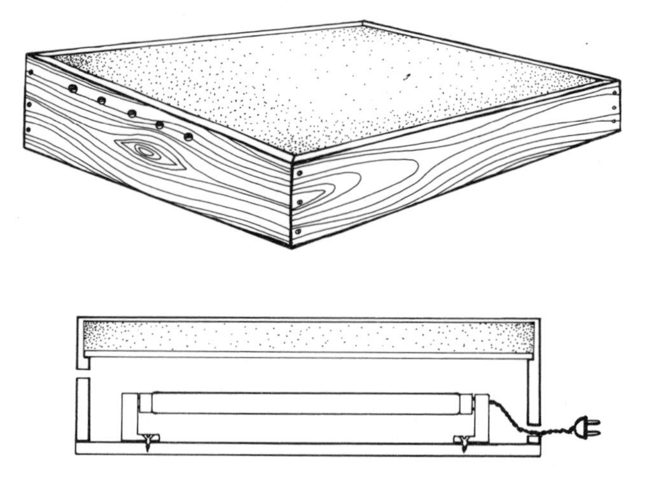

Fig. 38. Light box for painting 'opaque' designs

Painted designs have both freedoms and restrictions. With designs consisting of bold areas of colour and medium-size details, any brush will be found useful for painting. With designs of a more complex and detailed construction it will be found necessary to outline the shapes with a pen and indian ink, then to fill in these shapes with opaque paint. When using ink, care must be taken to see that the entire line drawn is opaque; it will often be found necessary to draw over the line for a second time after the first application is dry.

All qualities normally associated with painting may be created for screen printing: designs built up from various brushstrokes, stippled, stencilled and textured effects, freely shaped designs and tight, well-defined designs may all be made by painting opaque on the transparent film.

Designs may also be scratched, through an area of painted 'opaque'. This may give good results for textured designs or ideas that consist solely of fine line work.

Designs from opaque materials

Any material will be found useful in creating a design, if it is laid directly on the 5-Star film and exposed to light. This procedure does not require a positive transparency. Such things as leaves, cut-paper shapes, fabrics, lace etc. will give exciting results. Care must be taken when using these materials that they are opaque; if they are not, they may be made so by painting or rolling them over with 'opaque'. Rich and varied results may be obtained using a combination of painted and drawn motifs and opaque sheet materials.

When exposing 5-Star film to light with opaque sheet materials, it is advisable to hold the design firmly to the film with a sheet of glass.

Photographs

Photographs may be used for silk-screening designs if all the tonal variations are interpreted in terms of black and white or positive and negative. The use of 'line-film' is the most direct way of doing this (Kodalith or Formolith). The results from using line-film are usually bold and eye catching, consisting as they do of large areas of colour plus all tonal effects being reduced to rich textures of positive and negative value.

A photographic darkroom is absolutely necessary for this technique, equipped with enlarger, developing trays etc., and some knowledge of photography is necessary, but this can be very basic.

Ceramic printing inks

As with all ceramic techniques, the materials used must be able to withstand the heat of firing in the kiln. There is no difference between the basic materials used for ceramic silk-screening and any other ceramic decorating technique. Colours in ceramic techniques are gained through using various metallic oxides either singly or in some combination. Ceramic printing inks may be made from any of these basic metallic oxides, used by themselves or in combination one with another.

A general division of these materials regarding their properties is as follows:

1. Enamels—firing at 700°C.–800°C.
2. Pigments—firing at 800°C.–1,250°C.
3. Glazes—firing at 900°C.–1,250°C.

All these materials may be screen-printed when specially prepared and mixed with a screen-printing oil medium.

ENAMELS 700°C.–800°C.

Enamels may be purchased ready to use, mixed with screen-printing medium.

They are designed to be printed directly to a fired glaze surface or to a decal paper for making transfers.

The fired quality of enamel colours is dense and smooth, consistent in colour and edge definition. These qualities make enamels excellent colours for screen printing. They are suitable for printing both large bold areas of colour and small fine details. As they retain their edge value when printed and fired, they are good for multicolour prints where accurate registration is necessary.

They are normally printed as single deposits of colour. There is, however, no reason why overprinting should not be attempted, providing that experiment shows it to be successful.

Some unusual ways of using enamels are as follows; it should be remembered that experiment must precede actual work if success is to be guaranteed.

1. Enamels are usually fired at temperatures between 700°C.–800°C. If, however, this temperature is raised up to approximately 900°C., colour changes take place that may prove useful in some designs. The quality of the fired enamel may also be altered by overfiring. Colours that are normally flat and opaque may become transparent and uneven in colour.
2. Most enamel designs are carried out on a white glazed background. This is so that the colour and quality of the enamels show to best advantage and the chemical make-up of the enamel is unaltered. There is no reason why enamels should not be printed on coloured glaze backgrounds, providing the following are considered.

(a) Some strongly coloured glazes will interfere with the colour of the enamel, modifying and at times completely destroying the enamel's intended colour.
(b) The visual colour value of the enamel may be altered due to the proximity of a large area of another colour.

3. Enamels may, if needed, be used on biscuit tiles. If this is done, their firing temperature should be raised by 10°C.–20°C.
4. Enamels may give interesting effects if used as underglaze colours.
5. Intermixing enamels may prove successful and some types are designed to do this. It must be stated once more, that if any of these unconventional methods are used, experiments are necessary to prove their worth.

PIGMENTS 900°C.–1,250°C.

The word 'pigment' may be interpreted in many ways; for the purposes of this chapter it may be interpreted as follows:

One or more of the basic metallic oxides mixed with screen-printing medium and used for printing on a glazed fired surface, a biscuit surface or a decal transfer paper.

It may be fired at any temperature suitable for the surface on to which it is deposited.

Pigments or metallic oxides usually give muted colours ranging from metallic blacks and browns to dark blues and greens. To heighten the brilliance and clarity of their colour it will be found necessary to either dilute them and disperse their colour, by the addition of a small amount of glaze, or to print a very thin layer of pigment which will be dispersed by the glaze surface on which they are deposited. An example of a pigment is as follows:

4 parts cobalt carbonate
1 part tin oxide
2 parts glaze frit

The result of firing this pigment on to the surface of a white glaze would be:

a dark blue colour tending to have a matt surface.

The ingredients play the following roles:

Cobalt carbonate: the main body of the pigment giving the blue colour.

Tin oxide disperses and lightens the blue colour.

Glaze frit: fluxing agent which bonds the oxides together and helps promote adhesion to tile's surface.

The advantages that may be gained by using pigments are as follows:

1. They may be made to fire at any temperature.
2. Their 'earthy' quality is one which fits some designs better than the clarity of enamels.
3. They may be successfully printed over or under a glaze.
4. They can be used in designs where variations in finished results (accidental effects) are desired.
5. Fired qualities are nearer to 'handmade' pottery than to industrially made pottery.

SCREEN-PRINTED GLAZES 900°C.–1,250°C.

Any glaze may be screen printed, providing the following conditions are acceptable to the design and studio conditions:

1. Possible loss or change of colour intensity due, to a lessening of the thickness of glaze deposited. This is especially true of stoneware glazes.
2. Loss of fine details in design which results when glaze fluxes in firing.
3. Loss of fine details in design due to need for a very coarse fabric mesh size.
4. The glaze must be of a finer particle size than for normal application. It will be necessary to grind glaze in a ball mill to achieve the best results.

When preparing a glaze for screen printing it should be mixed in the usual way, e.g. ingredient weighed, mixed with water and sieved. It should then be dried completely and mixed with screen-printing oil medium.

Generally, glazes should only be screened directly to a tile's surface, which may be glazed or biscuit. Small designs can with some difficulty be printed as transfers. The problem in making glaze transfers comes with the additional thickness in the deposit of material. This tends to brush off the decal paper when the work is transferred to the ware.

Mixing colours for screen printing

If ready-mixed enamels are used for screen printing, care must be taken to see that the enamel has not separated from the oil medium. Before use, the whole contents of the container should be thoroughly stirred. Some colours tend to settle to the bottom of the container and form quite solid lumps; these must always be mixed with the oil if proper results are to be obtained.

If powdered enamels are to be mixed with printing oil, the proper consistency is that of thick syrup, which will run off a palette knife in a continuous but slow-moving stream. This rule applies to all types of ceramic printing inks, enamels, glazes and pigments.

Any thinning of ceramic inks should be carried out by adding more oil medium and never by adding turpentine or white spirit which has the effect of breaking the oil down and interfering with its printing quality.

The colour and oil should be mixed with either a palette knife and palette or a mortar and pestle.

The mixed colour should be passed through a fine sieve; this is a messy business and provided the enamel, glaze or pigment powders are quite dry and finely ground, it is not absolutely necessary.

Taking the screen print

The method of printing ceramic inks is the same as for other types of silk-screen printing but with the following provisions:

1. The screen must be supported above the surface of the tile or decal paper, with a gap between fabric and tile or paper surface of approximately $\frac{1}{16}$ in. (Fig. 30a).
2. Only one stroke of the squeegee is necessary; any more strokes will smudge the design.

These two rules apply because the surface on to which the print is placed is not normally absorbent and the deposit of ceramic colour has to have a regulated thickness in order to work satisfactorily when fired.

Firing screen-printed tiles

As with any other type of tilework the initial rise in firing temperature should be slow and even. The slow rise in temperature is absolutely necessary with screened designs, as it allows the printing medium to burn away without distorting the design. When transfers are fired, both the medium and the plastic support that is necessary for transfers has to be burnt away.

In burning the oil medium away, it is possible to set up reduction conditions in the kiln; it is therefore necessary to ensure good ventilation of the kiln—without making draughts.

Straightforward print on white tile in blue enamel. Design taken from an original wood-cut by Mr. William Walker, Lecturer at Loughborough College of Art. Printed by the author

Printed on a sheet of window glass which was subsequently fired on to the tile's surface, creating textures and distortion of the original drawing

8 · Mixed Techniques in Making and Decorating Tiles

In previous chapters are to be found the basic techniques for decorating and making tiles. These techniques will individually give great scope for design and personal expression. They will each be found to have a 'rightness' for any one particular design or idea. When using any single technique, problems may be encountered which will be found to be either difficult or impossible to solve within the terms and qualities given by the single technique. At this point it should be remembered that there is no golden rule that precludes the use of other techniques or any part of other techniques to solve the problem.

Perhaps an example of this would be as follows—the design to be executed demands both muted colours and quality plus fine, precise detail in a bright range of colour. In this case it will be obvious that a stoneware glaze will give muted colours and interesting surface quality, but it will not give fine detail in bright colour. The materials and techniques associated with these requirements are to be found when enamels are used at low temperatures. The conclusion we must draw from these facts is that both stoneware and enamel materials must be used. It is at this point that preconcepts appear; it is traditionally unusual to use these two techniques together—it is, however, not unknown. The success of this venture, as with any other that requires mixed techniques, depends on the balance of the contributions given by the component techniques, and the imagination and creativity applied to make them successful.

Some of the following suggestions for mixed techniques may help in solving problems of this nature.

Glaze and enamel

The larger areas of colour are laid on the tile in glazes, by spraying, brushing etc. These are fired and further colours in enamels are applied by any means—silk-screen, painting etc. The two main qualities used here are:

1. The soft glassy colour of glaze.
2. The opaque, dense colour of enamel.

To have success with these two qualities, a decision must be reached as to their relationship. Is the glaze or the enamel to play a dominant role? What is the desired quality of the finished overall effect? How are the shapes, line, textures etc. in the design best achieved, with glaze or enamel? In what order should they be done? This last question is always present with mixed techniques and the answer is always the same—The technique demanding the highest firing temperature should always be completed first. In this way subsequent firings of different temperatures will not interfere or destroy the initial work.

In this glaze plus enamel example the glazed part of the work must be completed first and fired at the required temperature, then the enamels are added and fired at their lower temperature.

Coloured clay slips and coloured glazes

The normal use of coloured slips involve the whole of the design being completed in the slip and finished, after biscuit firing, with a coating of transparent glaze. The technique makes use of the colour palette existing in whatever number of slips are available. If we use coloured glazes to complete the design, then the colour palette is enlarged. The resulting colours are gained by the slip and by the glaze, plus the colour change that takes place when using a coloured transparent glaze over a coloured slip, e.g. a yellow glaze over a blue slip will give a green colour.

It will be seen from this simple example, that more planning is necessary before work commences with mixed techniques, than with single techniques.

Underglaze and on-glaze

The use of these two forms of decoration can create the illusion of depth in a design. The reason for this is that one statement is separated from another by the thin yet tangible layer of glaze. The qualities of each technique also contribute to this depth—underglaze work is invariably softened by the glaze covering it, while on-glaze decoration, whether majolica or enamels, is on top of the glaze and therefore more distinct. This difference in quality equals the visual effect of perspective—less definition in the distance and more definition in the foreground. This is not to say that these two techniques used together produce only depth; they also create a richer set of values than perhaps either one may do when used separately.

Screen printing and hand painting

The basic value of a screen-printed image is that it may be faithfully reproduced many times. The hand-painting technique is one which mainly concerns individual qualities that are not easily reproduced and are used for their variety. Put these two techniques together and we may produce work that is efficiently reproduced and contains elements of choice, personal discretion and variety. The use of 'mass production' plus personal skills is an old practice and may be seen on many nineteenth-century tiles, where copper plate engraved designs have been transferred to the tile's surface and hand-painted details have been executed in enamels.

The choice of materials to use for both the printing and painting techniques is varied and depends on the design to be carried out, e.g. printed enamels and painted enamels, printed pigments and painted glazes, or printed glazes and painted enamels.

Modelled forms and graphic images

The usual content that tiles have is either completely three dimensional (relief work) or two dimensional (graphic work). There is no reason why the two areas should not be interwoven in some way, e.g. a tile is made which has a modelled form or areas which are raised in relief. Graphic images are applied to chosen areas of the relief and composed so that they work as one design.

Relief modelling and textured glazes

If a modelled tile is to be completed by glazing its surface, extra qualities may be added by choosing the right glaze. If we use a glaze which is decorative in its fired effect, e.g. textured in some way, we must ensure that the modelling and glaze qualities work together and do not destroy each other. The way in which we see form is concerned with tonal variations created by light falling on the form. In this way it is usual to see high points of the form as light tones and low points as darker tones. If the glaze applied to modelled surfaces interferes with this natural way of distinguishing form, then in all probability the modelling will be destroyed or camouflaged.

It is a good general rule to use textured glazes on modelled surfaces only when the glaze changes to a darker tone when applied in a thicker layer. When a glaze is poured over a modelled surface there is always a tendency for it to be deposited in thicker layers in the lower parts or details of the modelling.

Sgraffito with slips and glazes

The technique of sgraffito is traditionally associated with clay-slip work. There is, however, another application for sgraffito which will prove equally rewarding and that is scratching through a coating of glaze. The sgraffito design may be applied to a biscuit tile after glazing. This results in an unglazed line which shows as a matt surface after firing. If coloured slips are used on the tile, any sgraffito work carried out after glazing will reveal the true colour of the slip. Alternatively one may re-glaze a glazed and fired tile and use sgraffito through the second glaze to reveal the colour of the first glaze.

Cast tiles and hand-modelling

Cast tiles are identical one to another and this repetition can give rich surface qualities when the tiles are placed together. It is possible to add further interest to the design by modelling individual tiles after they have been made by slip casting or pressmoulding.

Slipcast tiles may prove to be the most difficult to use in this way, due to the nature of the clay slip, which tends to defy the normal behaviour of plastic clay, should it be dried to a more solid consistency for modelling. This very fact will give much scope for experiments and very interesting relief textures may be produced, together with some very peculiar modelled forms.

Pressmould tiles that are made from plastic clay do not give any problems. The surface of the repeated tile may be modified by modelling just as one chooses.

It should be seen from these examples that mixed techniques may enlarge the choice of qualities to be used in any design and increase one's versatility of expression and the convenience in carrying out a design.

9 · Factory-made Tiles

As with most industrial products, the tile needs a complex organization of machines and skills for its successful manufacture.

The simplicity of a tile's shape, finish and use, tends to obscure the amount of energy expended in its production.

Basic skills and knowledge are always necessary to make a ceramic object. The more specialized the ceramic object, the more special are the skills and knowledge necessary for the object's completion. The tile industry requires all the skills known to the potter concerning clays, glazes, kilns etc. These skills then have to be modified in order that they should produce the special object: the tile. The tile industry does not, therefore, differ in any way from the general pottery industry, other than in its special product.

The production of a tile must commence with the treatment of the raw materials, clay and glazes, and continue along its special path as may be seen in diagrammatic form (Fig. 39).

The factors which create the need for a complex organization are generally as follows:

1. An almost infinite number of tiles have to be made, all reproduced exactly.
2. Control must be exercised over quantities and continuity of quality.
3. Any one tile must be an economic success.
4. Both technical and aesthetic values must be considered.
5. The tile must be sold to the public; this involves marketing and advertising techniques.

All the points above are interdependent and to see this clearly we must look at each in detail.

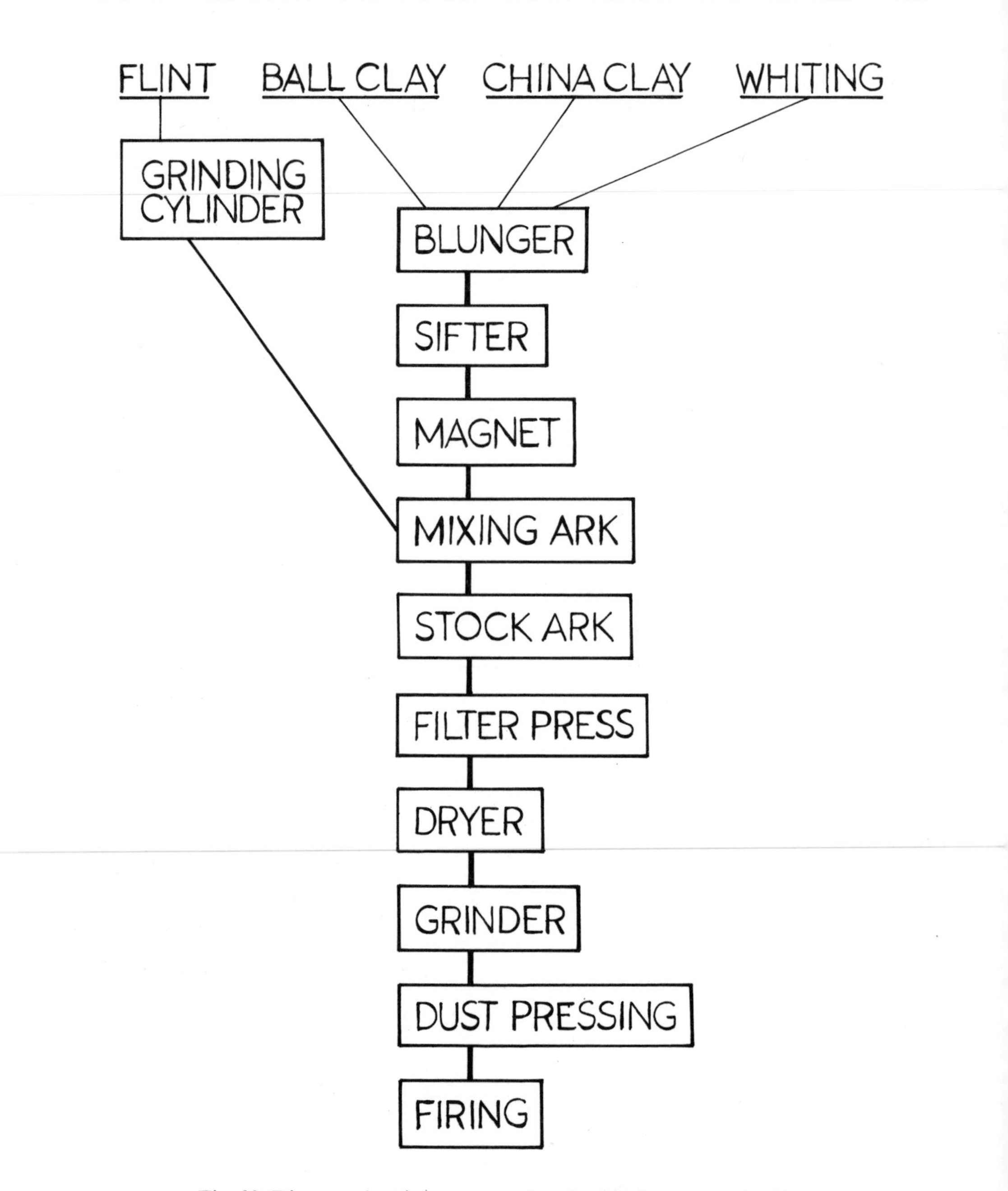

Fig. 39. Diagram showing processes involved in factory-made tiles

1. *The number of tiles to be made*

The number of tiles made in any one design depends on the proven value of the tile in use and in manufacture. It may be deduced from this that plain white tiles will have great advantage, followed by plain tiles of other colours.

Tiles having decoration or a special shape will be useful only as long as its design fits any given situation; in this way its production will probably be on a smaller scale than plain tiles.

The number of designs made at any one time by one factory depends on the amount of material, machinery and manpower at the disposal of the factory.

2. *Quality and quantity control*

Quality is always the outcome of the skills employed in manufacture. Quantity is dependent on point (1) and on the degree to which skills are selected and employed.

3. *Economic success*

Without profit the tile factory would cease to function, so all actions and decisions taken in the production of a tile must be considered in the light of economy.

4. *Consideration of technical and aesthetic values*

These two values should always be made to work together. From any point of view it would be wrong to produce a tile which fell into pieces when used, no matter how good its aesthetic value. Equally so, it is wrong to produce a technically sound tile which we cannot bear to look at. There must always be a sound compromise between techniques and aesthetics.

5. *Marketing and advertising*

After all the complexity of manufacture has been worked through and a product achieved, people must be able to acquire and use the tile. Much of the success in marketing depends on the tile's aesthetic value and its proven technical qualities. The advertising and marketing of a tile therefore relies heavily on the quality of the product. It is absolutely impossible to create a design that pleases everyone, but it is possible to co-ordinate all facets of tile manufacture to a point where a satisfactory conclusion is reached, one that suits most tastes.

Complete freedom in choice of technique and design can never be exercised in factory conditions; this is best left to the individual potter who is making tiles for a small group in society, working to a commission or who is just pleasing himself, whatever the outcome. One possible summary of the situation is this—The tile industry cannot afford to experiment continually in all directions, or it would fail in its main concern. The studio potter cannot afford to exclude experiment, or he would fail in his main concern.

Techniques used in tile factories

DUST-PRESSED TILES

The majority of factory-made tiles are produced by the dust-pressing technique. This process involves the use of a powerful press and powdered clay.

The design of the tile is made in the form of a metal die or mould. This mould is made in two halves representing the front and the back of the tile.

The mould is fixed to a press and powdered clay is compressed under high pressure between the upper and lower halves of the mould (Fig. 40). The presses used in this technique may be either fully automated, or may involve some control by an operator.

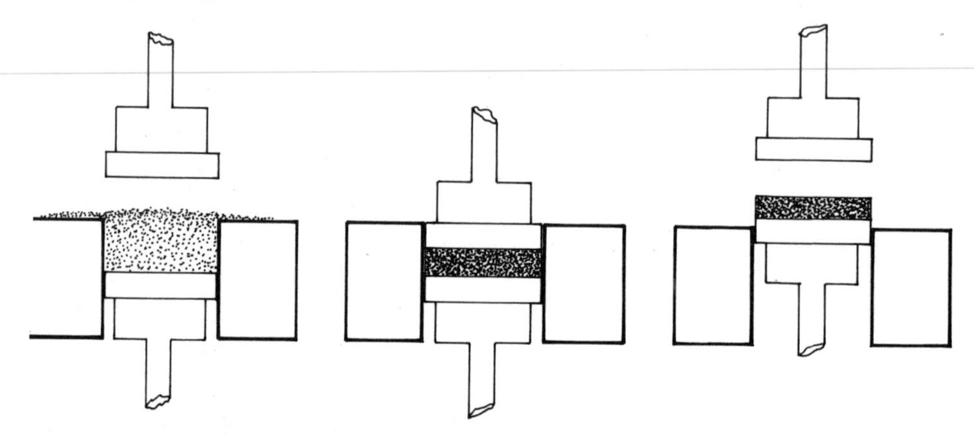

Fig. 40. Dust-press moulding

The pressure applied by the press is sufficient to bind the particles of powdered clay tightly together and retain the shape of the tile. The strength of the unfired dust-pressed tile is sufficient to allow the tiles to be stacked one on another in 3 ft. to 4 ft. tall columns when biscuit fired. This technique overcomes such problems found in drying plastic clay tiles, warpage etc. It is also possible to reproduce large numbers of tiles with great accuracy from one mould and press.

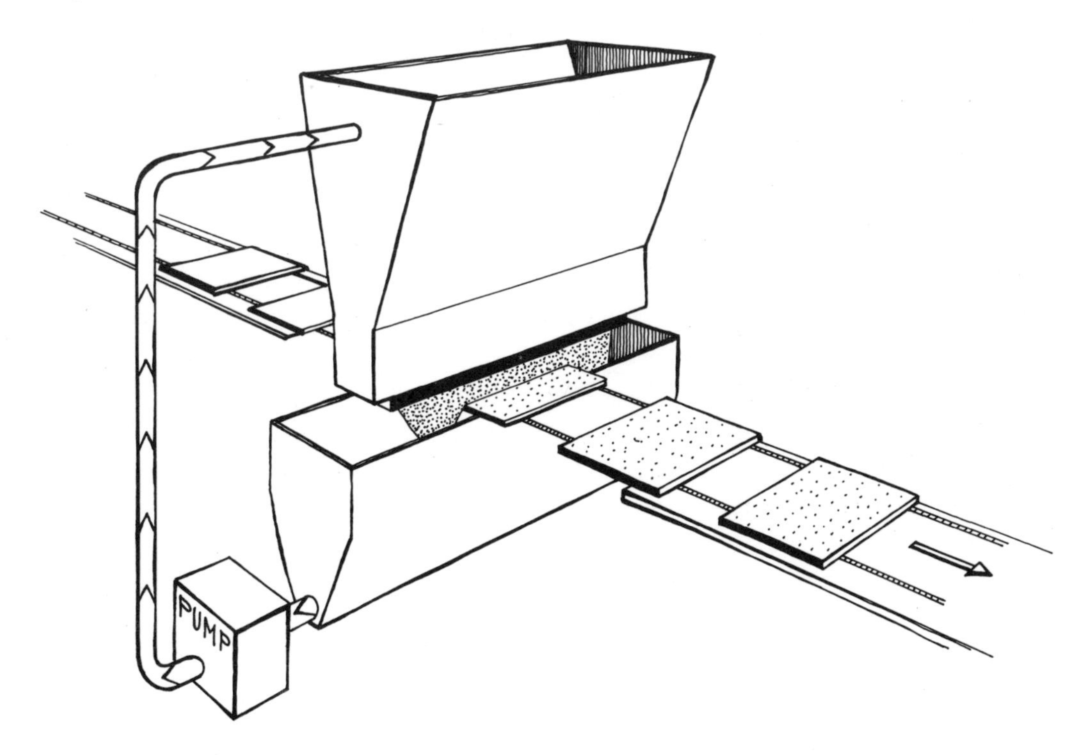

Fig. 41. Waterfall glazing

After biscuit firing, normally carried out at temperatures around 1,150°C., the tiles are placed individually on a conveyor belt system that carries them through a 'waterfall' glazing machine (Fig. 41). They are then packed in tile cranks, ready for the glost firing.

The kilns used to fire dust-pressed tiles are a continuation of the conveyor belt system, being tunnel kilns. These kilns are fired continually. The tiles are placed on trolleys and enter a tunnel. They move slowly through the tunnel, being first warmed, then fired and finally cooled in one slow movement, taking a period of up to two days for completion, depending on the type of firing cycle used.

EXTRUDED TILES

The basis of this technique is described in Chapter 3. There is little difference when it is used in industry, apart from the size of the extrusion machines and dies. Tiles made in this way include types of floor and roof tiles and other special cladding tiles, where strict reproduction of size or finish is not found necessary.

CAST TILES

Only the very largest of cladding tiles and special designs are made by this technique, whether it be slipcast or pressmoulded. Most industrially-cast tiles are solid and are usually made from heavily grogged thick slip.

Due to their size and weight these tiles have to be packed into a kiln as separate pieces, in a way which excludes the chance of warping or other faults.

Decoration of factory-made tiles

Decoration applied to mass-produced tiles is generally done in one of three ways.

1. Screen-printed on biscuit or glazed tile.
2. Relief designs worked into the moulds.
3. Decoration with glaze.

SCREEN-PRINTED DECORATION

Most screened designs are applied to the tile in a completely automatic way. The operator concerned with the technique need only check on the correct functioning of the printing machine. Designs are created either on the biscuit tile or on the glost tile. In either case the printing technique is the same, only the ceramic inks change.

Fig. 42. Relief tiles made by Candy Tiles Ltd., Devon

RELIEF DESIGNS

This type of decoration is very suitable for the mass-production techniques. The design may be built into the initial act of making the tile, e.g. dust-pressing or casting.

This saves the time and expense involved by having to decorate with another completely different technique. Generally speaking, in recent years the relief modelled tile has shown more scope for creativity in the tile industry than that shown when screen printing is used. This may, in part, be due to the direct method by which the tile is made, i.e. tile and decoration are made at the same time.

THE USE OF GLAZE AS DECORATION

Textured glazes can create interesting patterns over a tile's surface. The effects are usually accidental, but if and when they are controlled they may be used successfully for mass production.

These three main areas for decoration may at times be used together, with great success, as shown in the tiles made by Candy Tiles Ltd., of Devon, where strong relief work is combined with richly textured glazes (Fig. 42).

The tile industry is capable of creating any design in any technique, but for reasons of economy etc. it can never cater for all qualities or standards. Only the individual studio potters can fulfil the demands that are made on tiles as an expressive medium.

Fig. 42

Fig. 43. *above* Panel of kitchen tiles. Designed and printed by Marianne Zara, A.T.D.
below Panel of kitchen tiles. Designed by author and made by screen printing and hand painting

Fig. 44. Bathroom tiles. Designed and printed by Marianne Zara, A.T.D.

Wall surfaces

A wall surface may be clad in tiles for either a practical purpose or a decorative effect. The finish which some tiles give can create a hard-wearing and clean surface. Tiles used in this manner are usually flat or at least they do not have any surface treatment that detracts from cleanliness or efficient wear, such as relief textures or detailed modelling. They may, however, be highly decorated in a technique that preserves their practicality. Tiles designed and made commercially for wall cladding have a complete range of features that enable them to be used in almost any given situation. They are designed for use externally or internally in an architectural setting and each setting has its own peculiar problems. External tiles have to be impervious to the weather. They have to

10 · Uses for the Tile

Tiles are the means by which a surface may be created. They are used to improve an existing surface, making that surface more practical and more pleasing to look at. The visual and practical aspects of a tile can never be separated but it is possible to decide, when designing a tile, which aspect to emphasize, or whether to make them equal. The tiles surrounding a kitchen sink unit are there to fulfil the basic utility of cleanliness; they may, of course, at the same time create a pleasing visual contribution to the kitchen's decor (Fig. 43). This example of a use to which a tile may be put, shows clearly that some decision has to be reached regarding the tile's content or design. Plain white tiles placed in a kitchen environment may produce a visually pleasing finish to a wall surface and add something to the decor. They could possibly add more by being coloured or decorated. The choice to decorate or not, will depend on the relationship the tiles have with their surroundings and use.

It is clear from this example that both the practical and visual values of a tile must be considered from the point of view of the total scheme in which they are used. From this we may see that unless we know the uses for which a tile may be employed, we cannot make designs which have a sound basis. The following list will provide a broad indication of the uses to which a tile may be put:

1. Wall surfaces, decorative and practical (Figs. 43, 44).
2. Floor surfaces, mainly practical with decoration if desired.
3. Furniture, tabletops, working surfaces, decoration.
4. Fireplaces (Fig. 47).
5. Signs or directions, shop fronts, door numbers etc. (Fig. 48).
6. Framing, mirrors, doors, etc.
7. Cladding objects to contribute to a visually interesting finish, boxes, lamp bases etc. (Fig. 45).
8. Pictures and areas of pure visual attraction (Fig. 46).
9. Areas of extra value which complement or decorate. Single tiles inserted into architectural settings etc. (Fig. 47).

resist frosts that could crack them and rain that could soak them, possibly releasing them from their position.

Tiles used internally do not have these particular problems, but they do share other problems which are solved by the designing and making of specially shaped tiles, which enable proper completion of an area of tilework. These special tiles include such shapes as those designed for covings, corners and edges etc. (Fig. 27). If any large area of wall tiling is undertaken, the possible use of these special shapes will have to be considered, especially if a decoration is to be applied to the tiles' surface. It may be added here that possibilities exist for the use of these special shapes by themselves, to create interesting tilework.

In the purely decorative use of tiles for a wall surface, the choice of finish and design is much freer than that involved with cleanliness and wear. There is in these circumstances no need to consider technicalities, except those concerned with the production of the tiles. Freely composed tiles may be applied to a wall's surface, only partially covering its area. Techniques may be employed in creating the decoration that would normally be excluded from a tile's design and the practical implications normally associated with cladding tiles. High

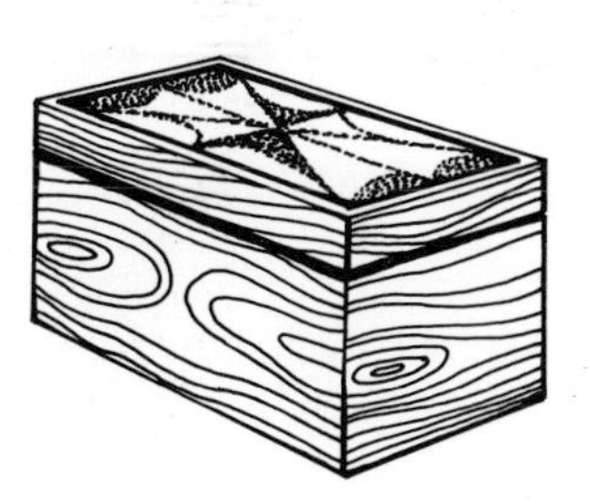

Fig. 45. Lamp base and box

Fig. 46. Picture of two heads. Designed and painted in glazes by Kenneth Gorman (*Photograph by courtesy of Durham County Schools Museum Service, Bowes Museum, Barnard Castle, Co. Durham*)

Fig. 47. Decorative tile work over a window on a 'Victorian' villa

relief work may be used, textured glazes and modelled surfaces may all be employed without fear of destroying the tiles' basic utility.

The only condition which still has to be considered if the work is designed for an external setting, is will it stand the weathering conditions? A tile used externally must be made impervious to moisture. If any moisture is absorbed by the tile and is subsequently attacked by frost, the ice so formed will expand and crack the tile. In industrial settings the polluted atmosphere may corrode a tile's surface. This is particularly true if soft earthenware glazes are used. The best external tiles are usually made in stoneware.

Floor surfaces

Unlike wall tiles, floors will always have the problem of their being a working surface. The considerations of wear, cleanliness and practicality always exist. It is no use at all making a floor surface over which it is impossible to walk. The only exception to this rule is that of surfaces which are protected in some way from access. Both the design and technique of floor tiles must conform to their basic use, e.g. it is useless glazing floor tiles with a low-temperature glaze which is soft after firing and so has no capacity to wear, or modelling the tiles' surface in such a way that one would trip over relief work.

Furniture

The most obvious application of tiles to furniture is that of their use for the surface of tables or working surfaces, e.g. kitchen worktop units. The design and technical considerations in making and decorating tiles for furniture are related to the exact use to which the furniture is to be put. In this way tiles for occasional coffee tables may be interpreted relatively freely when compared to kitchen cabinet working surfaces.

As has been stated previously, the most obvious use for tiles in furniture is associated with tables; there is, however, no reason why tiles should not be used to clad other items of furniture, e.g. garden patio chairs and stools; cupboard doors and drawer fronts; plant boxes etc.

Fireplaces

Fireplaces are traditionally accepted areas in which tiles are incorporated. The methods by which tiles are arranged and fixed around a fireplace are well known, but with a little imagination and creativity, new compositions may be achieved, ranging from the novel to the completely utilitarian.

Signs and directions

Due to the permanency of ceramic materials, tiles are excellent vehicles for carrying messages or giving information. Shop names and descriptions, door numbers and house nameplates are normally associated with this use (Fig. 48). Advertisements were once pronounced on tile panels, but with the ever increasing speed in the change of social habits, this use and many similar uses are not at present in demand.

Fig. 48. Door number plate, and tiles advertising beer and meat

Frames

Tiles may be used to frame some object in order to enhance its appearance, e.g. mirrors, pictures, doors, windows etc.

Cladding objects

Just as walls are clad with tiles, so may objects be clad. Furniture has already been mentioned and many other features and fittings in a household may be decorated or enlivened with a cladding of tiles. Lamp bases, if of a simple construction, may be made from tiles stuck to a wooden former. Storage boxes may have sides or lids covered by tiles (Fig. 45).

The main contribution that tiles can give when used in this way is the quality and colour of ceramic materials.

Pictures, murals, etc.

As one would paint a picture in oils on canvas, frame it and display it, so tiles may be used. These 'pictures' may be as physically movable as any oil painting or they may be integrated into the architectural setting as described in 'wall cladding' (Fig. 46).

Areas of extra value designed to complement or enrich

Tiles may be used singly or in number to simply enrich or liven a situation which is complete in itself. Tiles may be looked upon in this situation as 'a little extra'. A single decorated tile, when propped up on a shelf, can bring colour to a domestic environment. In this way tiles may be considered as objects in their own right, existing for no other reason than for their inherent qualities.

Tiles have existed for a considerable length of time. This fact points to their usefulness. Their continued usefulness depends on past traditions and the imagination and creativity that is presently placed on their design and function. When making and decorating tiles, success depends, as in all human endeavours, on the sensibilities, knowledge and perseverance of the person involved.

List of Suppliers

Podmore & Sons Ltd., Shelton, Stoke-on-Trent
Clays, Glazes, Frits, Colours and Stains, Kilns, Pugmills, Tools
Watts, Blake, Bearne Ltd., Newton Abbot, Devon
Stoneware and Earthenware Clays
Potclays Ltd., Copeland Street, Stoke-on-Trent
Stoneware and Earthenware Clays
Cafferata Ltd., Newark-on-Trent, Nottinghamshire
Potters Plaster, Plaster of Paris
Acme Marls, Clough Street, Hanley, Stoke-on-Trent
Kiln Furniture
Blythes Colour Works, Cresswell, Stoke-on-Trent
Glazes, Colours and Stains, Screen-printing Inks, Lustre
John Matthey Ltd., Ceramic Division, Hatton Garden, London
Screen-printing Inks, Enamels, Lustre, Liquid Gold and Silver
Sericol Group Ltd., 24 Parsons Green Lane, London, S.W.6
Silk-screening Equipment, Stencils, Squeegees, Fabrics, etc.

Bibliography

Tiles. A General History. Anne Berendsen. Faber & Faber.
A Guide to the Collection of Tiles. Arthur Lane. Victoria and Albert Museum.
Practical Pottery and Ceramics. Kenneth Clark. Studio Vista.
Ceramic Colours and Pottery Decoration. Kenneth Shaw. Maclaren.
Silk Screen Printing for The Artist. Roger Marsh. Tiranti.
Dictionary of Ceramics. A. E. Dodd. Newnes.
Early Netherlands Majolica. Bernard Rackham. Geoffrey Bles.
Colour Slides. S. Elliott. 10 Orford Road, Endon, Stoke-on-Trent.
Understanding Pottery Glazes. David Green. Faber.
Pottery and Ceramics. Ernst Rosenthal. Pelican Books.
Slipware: How To Make It. Dorothy Kemp. Faber.
English Delftware. F. H. Garner and Michael Archer. Faber.
Experimenting with Pottery. David Green. Faber.
Early Islamic Pottery. Arthur Lane. Faber.
Later Islamic Pottery. Arthur Lane. Faber.
Recipe Book For Glazes and Colours. F. Vieweger. Coburg.

Index